This is a book you
wont mind reading!
Just think, you
have all these
lovely places in
your power - to
walk thru or
send someone.

Love and
Thanks for you,

Evelyn & Alex

Invitation to
Japanese Gardens

お拝　庭見

お庭拝見
Invitation to
Japanese Gardens

Photographs by KIICHI ASANO

Commentary by GISEI TAKAKUWA

English adaptation by Richard F. Dickinson
and Nobunao Matsuyama

CHARLES E. TUTTLE COMPANY
Rutland, Vermont & Tokyo, Japan

Representatives
For Continental Europe:
BOXERBOOKS, INC., *Zurich*
For the British Isles:
PRENTICE-HALL INTERNATIONAL, INC., *London*
For Australasia:
PAUL FLESCH & CO., PTY. LTD., *Melbourne*
For Canada:
M. G. HURTIG, LTD., *Edmonton*

First English language edition produced for
Charles E. Tuttle Co. by Mitsumura Suiko Shoin,
publishers of the original Japanese language edition.

Published by the Charles E. Tuttle Company, Inc.
of Rutland, Vermont & Tokyo, Japan
with editorial offices at
Suido 1-chome, 2-6, Bunkyo-ku, Tokyo

Library of Congress Catalog Card No. 74-87788
Standard Book No. 8048 0708-6

First printing, 1970

Layout by Susumu Masunaka & Takahiro Shima
PRINTED IN JAPAN

Table of Contents

TABLE OF CONTENTS **2**

II : GARDENS IN OTHER DISTRICTS

III : INVITATION TO JAPANESE GARDENS

Location of Gardens in Japan

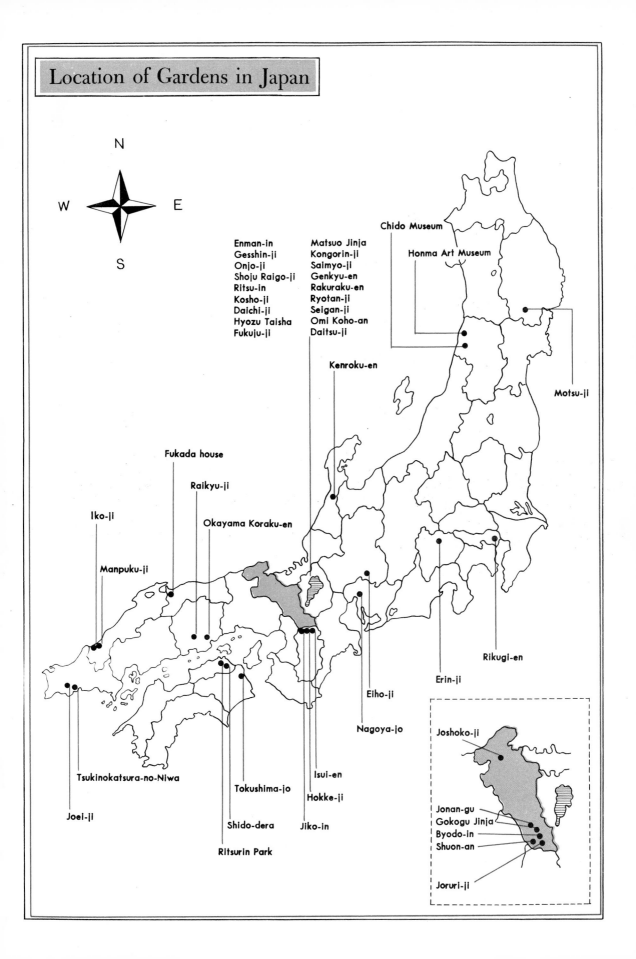

W   N   E
        S

Enman-in
Gesshin-ji
Onjo-ji
Shoju Raigo-ji
Ritsu-in
Kosho-ji
Daichi-ji
Hyozu Taisha
Fukuju-ji

Matsuo Jinja
Kongorin-ji
Saimyo-ji
Genkyu-en
Rakuraku-en
Ryotan-ji
Seigan-ji
Omi Koho-an
Daitsu-ji

Chido Museum
Honma Art Museum
Motsu-ji
Kenroku-en
Fukada house
Raikyu-ji
Iko-ji
Okayama Koraku-en
Manpuku-ji
Rikugi-en
Erin-ji
Eiho-ji
Nagoya-jo
Tsukinokatsura-no-Niwa
Tokushima-jo
Isui-en
Joei-ji
Shido-dera
Hokke-ji
Ritsurin Park
Jiko-in

Joshoko-ji
Jonan-gu
Gokogu Jinja
Byodo-in
Shuon-an
Joruri-ji

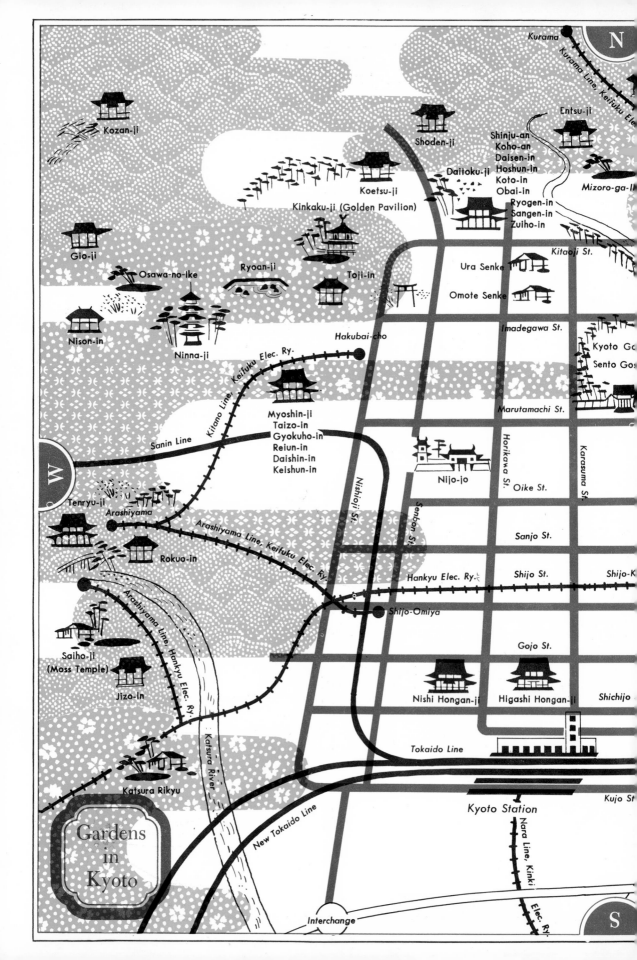

Gardens
in
Kyoto

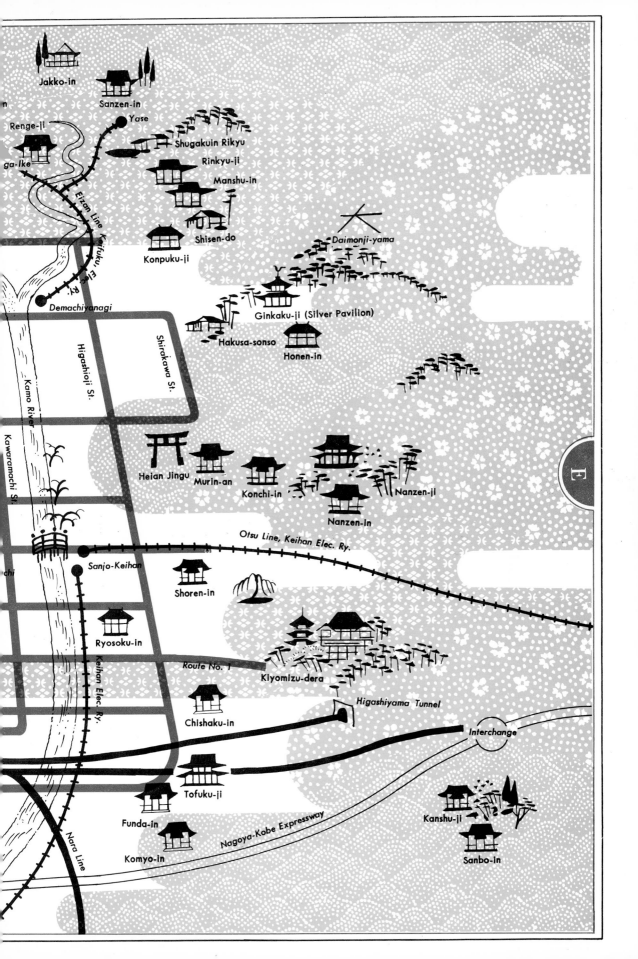

I : Gardens in Kyoto

Pond garden and dry landscape (*kare-sansui*) garden.
Constructed in the middle Edo period.
Kaisan-do gardens, Tofuku-ji temple.

Dry landscape garden.
Constructed in the Showa era by Shigemori Mirei.
North Garden, Abbot's Residence, Tofuku-ji temple.

Dry landscape garden.
Constructed in the Muromachi period according to tradition by Sesshu.
Repaired in the Showa era.
South Garden, Funda-in temple, Tofuku-ji temple compound.

Dry landscape garden.
Constructed in the Showa era by Shigemori Mirei.
Komyo-in temple, Tofuku-ji temple compound.

Pond garden for viewing from a building (*kansho-shiki*).
Constructed in the early Edo period according to tradition by the priest Unsho.
Chishaku-in temple.

Pond garden for viewing from a building.
Constructed in the early Edo period.
Joju-in garden, Kiyomizu-dera temple.

Pond garden for viewing from a building.
Constructed in the middle Edo period.
Garden of *shoin* building, Ryosoku-in temple, Kennin-ji temple compound.

16

Pond garden for viewing from a building.
Constructed in the early Edo period and repaired in the Meiji era.
Shoren-in temple.

Pond garden for strolling (*kaiyu-shiki*).
Constructed in the Taisho era by Ogawa Jihei.
East Garden, Heian Jingu shrine.

18

Pond garden for strolling.
Constructed in the Taisho era by Ogawa Jihei.
Central Garden, Heian Jingu shrine.

Dry landscape garden.
Constructed in the early Edo period
most likely by Kobori Enshu.
Garden for Abbot's Residence,
Nanzen-ji temple. ▲

Pond garden for viewing from a
building.
Constructed in the late Kamakura
period according to tradition by
Muso Kokushi.
Nanzen-in subtemple, Nanzen-ji temple
compound. ▶

20

Dry landscape garden.
Constructed in the early Edo period by Kobori Enshu and Kentei.
Konchi-in temple, Nanzen-ji temple compound.

Pond garden which incorporates a distant scene in its design (*shakkei*).
Constructed in the Meiji era by Ogawa Jihei.
Murin-an villa.

Pond garden with sand mounds.
Constructed in the middle Edo period.
Honen-in temple.

Pond garden for strolling.
Constructed in the Muromachi period by
Ashikaga Yoshimasa, Zen'ami, and others.
Ginkaku-ji temple (Silver Pavilion). ◀

Pond garden for strolling.
Constructed in the Taisho era by Hashi-
moto Kansetsu.
Hakusa-sonso villa. ▲

Northern Kyoto

Dry landscape garden with stream (*yari-mizu*).
Constructed in the early Edo period by Ishikawa Jozan.
Shisen-do villa.

Dry landscape garden.
Constructed in the late Edo period.
Konpuku-ji temple.

Dry landscape garden.
Constructed in the early Edo period by the priest-prince Ryosho.
Manshu-in temple.

Pond garden for viewing from a building.
Constructed in the early Edo period.
Rinkyu-ji temple.

Pond garden for strolling and boating (*sen'yushiki*).
Constructed in the early Edo period by the retired emperor Gomizunoö.

Upper Garden, Shugakuin Rikyu (Imperial Villa). ◀

Lower Garden, Shugakuin Rikyu (Imperial Villa). ▲

31

Pond garden for viewing from a building.
Constructed in the late Edo period.
Jakko-in temple.

Pond garden for viewing from a building.
Constructed in the Heian period and repaired in the Edo period.
Sanzen-in temple.

Dry landscape gardens.
Both constructed in the early Edo period.
Entsu-ji temple. ▲

Shoden-ji temple. ◢

Pond garden for strolling and viewing from a buiding.
Constructed in the early Edo period according to tradition by Jitsuzobo Jisshun.
Renge-ji temple. ▶

Pond garden for viewing from a building.
Date of construction unknown,
but believed to have been made by a man called Matashiro.
Jisso-in temple.

Teahouse garden (*roji*).
Date of construction unknown.
Koetsu-ji temple.

Koetsu-gaki fence.

37

Dry landscape garden.
Constructed in the Momoyama period according to tradition
by Asagiri Shimanosuke.
Kokei-no-Niwa garden, Nishi Hongan-ji temple.

Central
Kyoto

Pond garden for strolling.
Constructed in the early Edo period.
Tekisui-en garden, Nishi Hongan-ji temple.

Pond garden for strolling and boating.
Constructed in the Heian period.
Shosei-en villa, Higashi Hongan-ji temple.

Pond garden for strolling and viewing from a building.
Constructed in the Momoyama period.
Ni-no-maru, Nijo-jo Castle. ▲ ◀

41

Pond garden for strolling and viewing from a building.
Constructed in the early Edo period according to tradition by Kobori Enshu.
Oike-niwa garden, Kyoto Gosho (Imperial Palace). ◄

Pond garden for strolling.
Constructed in the early Edo period by Kobori Enshu.
Sento Gosho, Kyoto Gosho compound. ▲

Teahouse garden.
Constructed in the Momoyama period.
Omote Senke garden.

Teahouse garden.
Constructed in the early Edo period.
Ura Senke garden.

Dry landscape garden.
Constructed in the early Edo
period according to tradition by
the priest Ten'yu.
Daitoku-ji temple. ▲

Dry landscape garden.
Constructed in the Muromachi
period.
Shinju-an temple, Daitoku-ji
temple compound. ▶

46

Dry landscape garden.
Constructed in the early Edo period by Kobori Enshu.
Koho-an temple, Daitoku-ji temple compound.

Dry landscape garden.
Constructed in the Muromachi period by Kogaku Sodatsu.
Daisen-in temple, Daitoku-ji temple compound. ▲

Dry landscape garden.
Date of construction unknown.
Hoshun-in temple, Daitoku-ji temple compound. ▶

Dry landscape garden.
Date of construction unknown.
Koto-in temple, Daitoku-ji temple compound.

Dry landscape garden.
Constructed in the early Edo period.
Obai-in temple, Daitoku-ji temple compound.

Dry landscape garden.
Constructed in the Meiji era.
Sangen-in temple, Daitoku-ji temple compound.

Dry landscape garden.
Constructed in the Muromachi period.
Ryogen-in temple, Daitoku-ji temple compound.

Dry landscape garden.
Constructed in the Showa era by Shigemori.
Zuiho-in temple, Daitoku-ji temple compound.

Pond garden for boating.
Constructed in the Kamakura and Muromachi periods.
Kinkaku-ji temple (Gold Pavilion).

52

Western Kyoto

Dry landscape garden.
Constructed in the Muromachi period.
Ryoan-ji temple.

53

Pond garden for strolling.
The eastern section constructed in the Nanbokucho period according to tradition by Muso
Kokushi. The Fuyo-chi pond was constructed in the middle Edo period.
Toji-in temple.

Dry landscape garden.
Constructed in the Muromachi period according to tradition by Kano Motonobu.
Taizo-in temple, Myoshin-ji temple compound.

Dry landscape garden.
Constructed in the Momoyama period.
Gyokuho-in temple, Myoshin-ji
temple compound. ▲

Dry landscape garden.
Constructed in the Muromachi period.
Reiun-in temple, Myoshin-ji
temple compound. ▶

56

Dry landscape garden.
Constructed in the Muro-
machi period by Hosokawa
Masamoto.
Daishin-in temple, Myo-
shin-ji temple compound. ◀

Dry landscape garden.
Constructed in the early
Edo period according to
tradition by Gyokuenbo, a
disciple of Kobori Enshu.
Keishun-in temple, Myo-
shin-ji temple compound.▼

Pond garden for strolling and viewing
from a building.
Constructed in the early Edo period.
Ninna-ji temple. ▲

Pond garden boating.
Constructed in the Heian period.
Osawa-no-Ike pond. ▶

58

Pond garden for strolling and viewing
from a building.
Constructed in the Nanbokucho period by
Muso Kokushi.
Tenryu-ji temple. ▲

Dry landscape garden.
Constructed in the early Edo period.
Rokuo-in temple. ▶

Teahouse garden.
Constructed in the Showa era.
Nison-in temple.

Teahouse garden.
Constructed in the Meiji era.
Gio-ji temple.

Constructed in the Kamakura period.
Kozan-ji temple.

Pond garden.
Constructed in the Nanbokucho period.
Joshoko-ji temple.

Dry landscape garden.
Constructed in the Nanbokucho period by Muso Kokushi.
Saiho-ji temple (Moss temple). ▲

Pond garden for strolling.
Constructed in the Nanbokucho period by Muso Kokushi.
Ogon-chi pond, Saiho-ji temple. ◀

Dry landscape garden.
Constructed in the Muromachi period.
Jizo-in temple. ▶

Pond garden for strolling.
Constructed in the Momoyama period by Prince Toshihito and his son Toshitada.
Katsura Rikyu (Imperial Villa). ◀▲

Pond garden for strolling and dry landscape garden.
Constructed in the Showa era by Nakane Kinsaku.
Rakusui-en, Jonan-gu shrine.

Dry landscape garden.
Constructed in the Showa era by Nakane Kinsaku.
Gokogu Jinja shrine.

Pond garden for boating and a dry landscape garden in front of the study hall.
Constructed in the Heian period.
Kanshu-ji temple.

Garden for viewing from a building.
Constructed in the Momoyama period by Toyotomi Hideyoshi, Kentei, and others.
Sanbo-in temple.

Pond garden for viewing from a building.
Constructed in the Heian period.
Hoö-do hall, garden, Byodo-in temple.

Dry landscape garden.
Constructed in the early Edo period by Shokado Shojo,
Ishikawa Jozan, and Sagawada Kiroku.
Shuon-an temple.

Pond garden for strolling.
Constructed in the Heian period by Eshin (Izu-Sojo).
Joruri-ji temple.

II : Gardens in Other Districts

Pond garden for viewing from a building.
Constructed in the early Edo period.
Enman-in temple. ▲

Pond garden for strolling and viewing from a building,
Constructed in the early Edo period.
Gesshin-ji temple. ◣

Dry landscape garden.
Constructed in the Asuka period.
Onjo-ji temple. ▶

Dry landscape garden.
Constructed in the Momoyama period by Hoshinadera Soshin.
Shoju Raigo-ji temple. ▲

Garden with a flowing stream.
Constructed in the early Edo period.
Ritsu-in temple. ◣

Pond garden for strolling by a winding stream (*kyokusui-shiki*).
Constructed in the Muromachi period according to tradition by Hosokawa Takakuni.
Kosho-ji temple (formerly Shurin-ji temple). ▶

Dry landscape garden.
Constructed in the early Edo
period by Kobori Enshu.
Daichi-ji temple. ▲

Pond garden for strolling.
Constructed in the Kamakura
period.
Hyozu Taisha shrine. ▶

Pond garden for strolling.
Constructed in the early Edo period.
Fukuju-ji temple. ▶

Dry landscape garden.
Constructed in the Momoyama period.
Matsuo Jinja shrine.
▼

Pond garden for strolling and viewing from a building.
Constructed in the Momoyama and Edo periods.
Kongorin-ji temple.

Pond garden for strolling and viewing from a building.
Constructed in the early Edo period by the priest Yukan.
Saimyo-ji temple.

Pond garden for strolling and boating.
Constructed in the Momoyama period.
Genkyu-en garden.

Dry landscape garden.
Constructed in the early Edo period by a member of the Katori family.
Rakuraku-en garden.

Dry landscape garden.
88   Constructed in the early Edo period by the Zen priest Koten.
South Garden, Abbot's Residence, Ryotan-ji temple.

Pond garden for strolling and viewing from a building.
Constructed in the early Edo period by Koten.
Study Hall, Ryotan-ji temple. ◀

Dry landscape garden. ▼
Constructed in the early Edo period by a member of the Katori family.
Seigan-ji temple.

Dry landscape garden and pond garden.
Constructed in the middle Edo period..
Omi Koho-an temple.

Pond garden.
Constructed in the middle Edo period.
Daitsu-ji temple.

Dry landscape garden.
Constructed in the early Edo period by Katagiri Sekishu.
Jiko-in temple. ▲

Pond garden for strolling and viewing from a building.
Constructed in the early Edo period and also in the Meiji era.
Isui-en garden. ▶

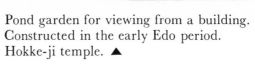

Pond garden for viewing from a building.
Constructed in the early Edo period.
Hokke-ji temple. ▲

Pond garden and dry landscape garden.
Constructed in the Momoyama period by Ueda Soko.
Senshu-kaku, Tokushima-jo Castle, Tokushima City.

Pond garden.
Constructed in the Muromachi period by Hosokawa Yoriyuki and remodeled in the
Showa era by Shigemori Mirei.
Shido-dera temple, Kagawa Prefecture.

Pond garden for strolling.
Constructed in the early Edo period.
Ritsurin Park, Takamatsu City.

Pond garden for strolling.
Constructed in the early Edo period by Tsuda Nagatada.
Okayama Koraku-en garden, Okayama City.

Dry landscape garden.
Constructed in the Momoyama period by Kobori Enshu.
Raikyu-ji temple, Takahashi City.

98

Pond garden for viewing from a building.
Constructed in the Kamakura period.
Fukada house garden, Yonago City.

Pond garden for strolling and viewing from a building.
Constructed in the Muromachi period according to tradition by Sesshu.
Iko-ji temple, Masuda City.

Pond garden for viewing from a building.
Constructed in the Muromachi period according to tradition by Sesshu.
Manpuku-ji temple, Masuda City.

Dry landscape garden.
Constructed in the middle Edo period by Katsura Tadaharu.
Tsukinokatsura-no-Niwa garden, Bofu City. ▲

Pond garden for strolling and dry landscape garden.
Constructed in the Muromachi period according to tradition by Sesshu.
Joei-ji temple, Yamaguchi City. ▶

Tohoku District

Pond garden for strolling.
Constructed in the Heian period.
Motsu-ji temple, Iwate Prefecture.

Pond garden for strolling.
Constructed in the late Edo period by Honma Kodo.
Honma Art Museum, Sakata City. ▲

Pond garden.
Constructed in the Edo period.
Chido Museum, Tsuruoka City. ▶

Ⅲ : Invitation to Japanese Gardens

WAY OF APPRECIATION

The more often one sees a particular garden and the more one studies it, the more profound it is discovered to be. This is of course true for everything, but particularly so for the garden. The reasons for this are many. Most gardens are out-of-doors and despite the differences of their sizes, they have suffered changes caused by the long years. Many gardens exist with no historical record, with others their originator or architect is unknown, and with many the date of creation is also unknown. To cite an example, in the Muromachi period (1393–1573) the Japanese garden reached its zenith and the garden of Saiho-ji temple, built in the Nanbokucho period (1333–93), took the lead. But specialists and students of the garden hold divergent views even on the period in which the Saiho-ji garden was made. Moreover, from the earliest beginnings many gardens have suffered much alteration.

It is often said that individual gardens are evolving incessantly in quality and sophistication. It is also true, however, that many gardens have disappeared as a result of damages incurred by typhoon and flood. In the basic work *Miyako Rinsen Meisho Zue* (Pictures of Famous Scenic Gardens of Kyoto), there are paintings of gardens which existed up to the year of publication (1799) but of these a considerable number were destroyed during a one hundred and fifty year span between this date and the present. During the Meiji Restoration which began in 1868, in addition to the threat to Buddhism whereby many temples were demolished, to our great regret many gardens were likewise destroyed. Thus the garden has had a quite complicated and even strange history.

Temple gardens of the present are situated within the confines of the temple grounds and create for the temple an atmosphere of quiet beauty. The "dry landscape" (*kare-sansui*)

113

gardens of sand and rock of the Zen temples are places for meditation and discipline, and symbolic of Zen thought. These temple gardens have been handed down to us along with the histories of the temples themselves, and that they are open to us is a cause of great joy worthy of our respect and gratitude. While visiting a garden one should bear in mind that the payment of a fee does not of course grant any special privileges beyond the permission to enter. All visitors should also bear in mind that there are many who have come to the garden for meditation and thought, and respectful consideration toward them and even a certain amount of silence should be common conduct. The title of this book, *Invitation* conveys the idea that one has been invited to the garden and each person should try to love, protect, and preserve it.

THE HISTORY OF JAPANESE GARDENS

Heian Period (784–1192)

From which period and how was the Japanese garden first developed? The first document which contains reference to the garden is the *Nihon Shoki* (Chronicles of Japan, completed in 720). However, even before this time people made ponds dedicated to the gods and in addition they arranged rock piles in groups and combinations of stones called *iwakura* or *iwasaka,* these being regarded as divine manifestations. One of these larger *iwakura* can now be seen at Miwayama in Nara. Such combinations of stones or ponds, along with islands in the center of the ponds, mark the first beginnings of the Japanese garden. In the *Nihon Shoki* we find a reference to a divine pond where carp were released symbolically as an offering to the god of the pond. After the arrival of Buddhism into Japan in the sixth century the *kasan* (mound of earth) was introduced into Japanese gardens as an imitation of Mt. Shumisen, the highest mountain in the ideal world of Buddhism. This mound of earth is the forerunner of the present-day miniature hill of Japanese gardens.

During the reign of the Empress Suiko (554–628), Umako of the Soga clan had a pond with an island built on the grounds of his mansion. This is thought to be the first pond garden distinctly recognized as such.

Many other pond gardens, modeled after the garden of Umako, were made in the Asuka period (552–645), the Nara period (710–84), and down through the Heian period. Most of them symbolize the vast ocean and seem to be the re-crea-

Rock within Akaiya of
Onjo-ji

Shizen-en, today

Bokakaku of Shosei-en

tion of the ideal world for which people of that age longed.
This same tendency has appeared in various ways in the gardens of later years, even in the dry landscape gardens of sand and rock. Unfortunately the pond gardens of the Asuka and Nara periods seldom exist today.

The stones around Akaiya building (p. 79) to the west of the Kondo hall of Onjo-ji temple in the city of Otsu, in Shiga Prefecture, are believed to be a part of the pond garden of the mansion of Prince Otomo Yota, a grandson of the Emperor Tenchi (626–71). They are perhaps the oldest of the *sanson* stones which stand for three Buddha images.

After the capital was moved to Kyoto by the Emperor Kanmu in 784, which marked the beginning of the Heian period, the garden developed rapidly.

There still exists to the south of Nijo Castle in Kyoto a portion of the first garden of the Heian period called Shizen-en. An Imperial garden within the grounds of the Emperor's palace, it was a large pond garden which made use of the natural configuration and ample water. Successive emperors of the early Heian period enjoyed with their followers massive parties on board large boats on this pond. Hunting and fishing were also favorite pastimes.

During the Heian period, Imperial gardens of large scale were built in many places. The only vestige which remains is Osawa-no-Ike pond (p. 59) while the others have been completely destroyed. Osawa-no-Ike pond was originally made from irrigation ponds made and used by the invited immigrants and their descendants from China called the Hata clan. It was in turn beautified and made into a lovely pond garden. Needless to say, a thousand years did much to alter the garden but still it remains today the oldest important vestige of the ancient gardens in Kyoto.

The next garden is that of Rokujo-Kawara-no-in villa of Prince Minamoto Toru (822–95), the son of the Emperor Saga who renounced his position in the Imperial family. Kawara-no-in is now called Shosei-en or Kikoku-tei villa.

Minamoto Toru loved Kawara-no-in villa so much that he was called Kawara-Sadaijin (the minister of the left). It is said that he made his garden look like Shiogama of the Tohoku district where salt was extracted, and sent for salt water from Naniwa (the present Osaka) and enjoyed watching the people work to obtain salt from the salt water. What this legend tells us is that the garden pond stood for the sea and a part of the garden was used for making salt.

The main attraction of Shosei-en villa is the Ingetsu-chi

Pond garden of Kanshu-ji

Shinden style of architecture and pond garden

pond which occupies the southeastern part of the whole garden (p. 40). A large island in the southern area of the pond is the paradise island and a gigantic rock standing conspicuously on the beach symbolizes the *horai* paradise. There are two islands of rock on the eastern side of the pond which are now in ruins but they are believed to have been made in the early Heian period.

The pond garden of Kanshu-ji temple at Yamashina is also worth noticing as an example of the early Heian period. The *shoin* (study room or hall) of the temple, Kanshu-ji, was formerly the grand hall used by the Emperor Meisei and is famous for the painting by Tosa Mitsuoki and the special gold inlaid *tokonoma* shelf called Kanshu-ji Dana. The hall looks out on a garden (p. 72) which was built after the *shoin* hall. It is small but beautiful with a stone lantern to the left as the focal point of the scene along with lovely stones and shrubbery and a low hedge which separates the garden from the pond which can be seen in the background. The shrubbery which covers the ground is the rare plant *haibyakushin* and presents a lovely sight.

One of the most conspicuous characteristics of the gardens of the early Heian period is their founder's selection of the most suitable pieces of land for their location, making use of the finest natural scenery of the Heian capital, at a time when the natural beauty was far more in abundance that it is today. The best example of such selection is Osawa-no-Ike. Another characteristic is to imitate a natural scene, such as the garden of Kawara-no-in villa imitating Shiogama as mentioned above. These two characteristics were handed down to the garden makers of later periods.

The mansions of nobles in the Heian period were constructed in the *shinden* style of architecture. The central building (*shinden*) faced a large pond into which flowed a stream and waterfall. This was the product not only of a sense of beauty but was well in accord with the luxurious mode of living of that age. The nobles of the Emperor's Court possessed elegant taste both in their mansions and in the gardens surrounding them. Here they entertained other nobles and were entertained by those who performed such acts as water tricks from China. Generally the main characteristic of the gardens of the Heian period is that they were places of enjoyment for court nobles.

The gardens of the Heian period were greatly influenced by the Buddhist Jodo faith (Pure Land faith) which gained great power in the middle of this period around the tenth century. A large amount of space cannot be given to the course

Image of Amida within Hoö-do

of its development, but the essential Jodo idea was the transiency of this world and the expected paradise in the next world. Men of that age believed strongly in salvation by Amida Buddha, believing more in the next world than in this one.

Michinaga and others in power at that time built elaborately decorated halls and dedicated them to Amida Buddha. In addition they attempted to make a garden with a lotus pond in imitation of the pond of the seven treasures of paradise, an attempt to recreate paradise in this world. The most representative remaining example of this trend is Hoö-do hall of Byodo-in temple (p. 74).

The temple of Joruri-ji, at Nishio, Kamo-cho, Minamiyamashiro (p. 76) gives an unforgettable impression to visitors. The pond and spring of this temple were built in 1150 by the Buddhist priest Eshin of Ichijo-in temple, Kofuku-ji temple in Nara. On the western side of the pond stands the central hall in which nine statues of Amida Buddha are enshrined. In the three-storied pagoda on the mound to the east of the pond is enshrined a Buddhist statue, Yakushi-Nyorai, which was once the principal image of the temple. The contrast between the central hall on the west and the pagoda on the east is a contrast between the Western Paradise (Jodo, Pure Land) and the Eastern Paradise (Joruri, Jewel of Paradise) with the garden pond in the middle serving as the lotus pond of Jodo.

Along with Byodo-in and Joruri-ji temples there exists another lovely garden at Hiraizumi in the northern section of Honshu, the garden of Motsu-ji temple (p. 109). The temple was modeled after the famous Chuson-ji temple and it is thought that it was made splendid in every way by the son of Motohira. Unfortunately the temple was completely destroyed and only the large garden pond, the island, and set of stones remain now as they were years ago and suggest that the garden was a typical example of the Jodo style of garden in both scale and structure.

The influence of Buddhism on the Japanese garden began with the Shumisen of the Asuka period as mentioned above, but the influence was more noticeable in the above-mentioned Jodo gardens, for they attempted openly to create a Jodo paradise. The philosophy of paradise which appeared in the garden was inherited by later gardens, such as the lower garden at Saiho-ji temple, where we find the Shinji-Ike pond (laid out according to the Chinese character, heart 心). Also the temple of Gold Pavilion, which was built in imitation of Saiho-ji, and a part of the garden of the temple of Silver Pavilion, where one finds a lotus pond which represents the seven treasures of

Hagitsubo of Kyoto Gosho

paradise. In the Kamakura and Muromachi periods the philosophy of Zen Buddhism was already influencing the gardens, but at the same time, those gardens also reflected the influence of Jodo-paradise thought. This tendency continued up to the Edo period.

Finally it should be noted that the style of the Heian-period gardens is still reflected in the style of the gardens in the Kyoto Imperial Palace, such as the southern garden of Shishinden hall, the eastern garden of Seiryo-den hall, and the Hagitsubo garden behind it.

Kamakura (1192-1333) and Nanbokucho (1333-93) Periods

The most characteristic element of the Kamakura period was that political power shifted from the aristocrats to the warrior class. However, the center of culture remained in Kyoto and its influence spread to the local areas, and gradually this Kyoto culture spread throughout the whole country. At the same time the spreading of the new sects of Buddhism further increased this tendency. In addition the import of Zen Buddhism by Eisai and Dogen and the visits of Zen priests from China greatly influenced the culture. As far as the gardens are concerned they still reflected the garden style of the previous period. Visitors to Ryoan-ji rock garden soon notice a quiet, large pond on the right of the main temple gate. This pond is called Kyoyo-chi (pond of the mirror) and this was formerly the garden pond of Gotokudaiji Sanesada's villa. It still has a central island which reminds visitors of the *sen'yu* style pond of that age, that is, a pond for boating amusement. This garden has played an important role in adding a sophisticated touch to the compound of Ryoan-ji. The teahouse beside the pond conveys the appearance of a Tsuri-dono (a viewing house beside a pond of the Heian period).

At the site of what is now Nanzen-ji temple, the retired emperor Kameyama constructed a villa. It was called Nanzen-in and had a pond garden (p. 20), which reflects the influence of Zen Buddhism, for many Zen temples were built at that time, that is to say, at the end of the Kamakura period. In addition to Nanzen-ji temple there is a garden in Saiho-ji temple which was made before Muso Kokushi entered the temple as head priest. It is said that there was also a pond garden in Kameyama-den villa which was the model for the later Tenryu-ji temple.

Outside of Kyoto there are a few other gardens of the Kamakura period which deserve mention. One of these is the garden of Shomyo-ji temple in the Kanazawa section of Yoko-hama, which is a typical Jodo-style garden. Another is the garden pond of Hyozu Taisha shrine (p. 82), an old shrine at Yasu in Shiga Prefecture. The garden of a Mr. Fukada in Yonago City, Tottori Prefecture, was also made in this period and its arrangement of stones on an artificial hill and the classical arrangement of crane and tortoise islands in the pond are worth noting (p. 99).

From the end of the Kamakura period down to the Nan-bokucho period the greatest influence on the garden came from Zen Buddhism. The *samurai* (warriors), who came into power replacing the nobles, observed the principles of simplic-ity and fortitude and became devout believers of Zen. From them Zen Buddhism was introduced into the court and soon after central temples of five sects of Zen were established in Kyoto and Kamakura, and Zen became influential on every level of culture and in every mode of life. Its influence natural-ly came to be felt and expressed in the garden. It was at this time that Muso Kokushi (1275–1351) appeared on the scene, a man destined to be the instrument by which this influence was felt in the garden. No record exists which relates how he acquired the art of garden construction but most probably his art was a natural gift enriched by his love of nature as a Zen priest.

Muso Kokushi

The garden of Saiho-ji temple with Ogon-chi pond as its center shows dynastic elegance and it is as beautiful as a Yamato-e painting. The scene is quite in keeping with what Muso's features suggest. However, the combination of the rocks in the dry garden and elsewhere in the upper garden is somewhat too dynamic to believe that they were set by the same architect who designed the lower garden. This is perhaps a cause of misunderstanding. I believe that in the heart of Muso there was the sense of elegance juxtaposed with a severe sense of the pursuit of the essence of Zen, which found expres-sion in the commanding aspect of the set of rocks. It is said that there is in every garden made by Muso a drooping cherry tree and a stone upon which to practice Zen meditation, or *zazen*. This is symbolic of the personality of Muso Kokushi. Needless to say, the natural scene with Ogon-chi pond as its center is not nature herself but supernature which has been unified by Muso's sense of beauty.

The Sogen-chi pond garden of Tenryu-ji temple was made by Muso Kokushi after the construction of the Saiho-ji garden, with a more refined and creative spirit. In addition to these two gardens two others have recently been attributed to

Muso's genius. These are the pond gardens of Toji-in and Nanzen-in temples, to which I will allude later when I refer to other gardens made by Muso in other areas.

Muromachi Period (1393-1573)

The gardens of this period mark an epoch in the history of the Japanese garden. In this period Zen Buddhism flourished even more than it had in the previous period and exerted an influence on every aspect of Japanese culture, giving birth to new learning, new art, and other accomplishments. Communication with China became active by means of trade and as a result many works of art and excellent paintings were imported. The influence of the North Sung style of painting using India ink to paint mountains and rivers had already appeared in the gardens of Tenryu-ji and in many other gardens. After the Onin Civil War the dry landscape garden was brought to perfection and its superb technique was demonstrated in the Zen temple gardens of Ryoan-ji and Daisen-in.

Prior to this, Ashikaga Yoshimitsu (1358-1409) had constructed Kitayama-den villa and had made a three-storied gold pavilion called Kinkaku. The large garden pond was used for boating by court nobles in the Heian style of amusement, with *horai* and *shinsen* islands in the pond. In front of the Gold Pavilion lotuses were planted in the style of a Jodo garden, bringing to mind Ogon-chi pond at Saiho-ji temple which also has the coloring of a Jodo-style garden.

Ashikaga Yoshimasa (1435-90), the eighth Shogun, built Higashiyama-den villa and made Kannon Hall, that is to say, the Silver Pavilion and many other halls in addition to the construction of a lotus pond for boating. However, due to the Onin Civil War the age of Yoshimasa was largely unproductive. However diligent he tried to devote himself to the construction of Higashiyama-den to the disregard of other affairs, he could not go beyond the Gold Pavilion in matters of economics and personal power. He did succeed in surrounding himself with men of significant accomplishment and established what was known as Higashiyama culture, which exerted a considerable influence on following ages.

As noted in regard to the villas of Gold Pavilion and Silver Pavilion, this period witnessed the construction of large garden ponds. Although these two villas were changed into Zen temples, they retained characteristics of the preceding period. After this time Zen-temple gardens were no longer constructed like that of the Silver Pavilion but were exclusively designed as "dry landscape" (*kare-sansui*) gardens. Two of the finest gardens ever built, which form a great contrast to each other in technique and style, still exist in Kyoto in the gardens of Ryoanji and Daisen-in temples. In addition to these, other Zen gardens are found in the subtemples within the compound of Daitoku-ji temple, as well as in the Myoshin-ji compound. Within the compound of Tofuku-ji temple there is a garden at Funda-in subtemple which is believed to be the work of Sesshu Toyo (1420–1506), a master painter and Zen monk. It is also believed that the garden of Rokuo-in temple was constructed in the early Muromachi period by Ninnanshu, as *ishitate-so,* that is, a priest of garden making.

Sesshu

Gardens of this period are also found in various places throughout the country but especially noteworthy are those believed to be by Sesshu which are found in the Chugoku, San'in, and Kyushu districts. Sesshu is well known as a great painter and priest. He first entered the priesthood in Bicchu, a province in western Japan, where he was born. He later came to Kyoto to serve at Shokoku-ji temple and was taught painting by Shubun. The gardens ascribed to him are to be found in Yamaguchi and the other places where he visited: Joei-ji temple in Yamaguchi, Manpuku-ji temple and Iko-ji temple of Masuda City in Shimane Prefecture and Kameishibo of Hikosan in Fukuoka Prefecture. Since each of the places where these gardens and temples exist were already related to Sesshu and since each garden is in the style of the North Sung paintings of mountains and rivers, besides being superb in artistic technique, I ascribe to the view that they were indeed all made by Sesshu. In Funda-in in Kyoto we find an example whereby modern architects used some beautiful rocks, which were all that remained of a garden built by Sesshu, to re-create a garden as nearly alike a typical Sesshu garden of an earlier time as possible.

Shiken Seido, a priest at Shokoku-ji temple and a successor to Sesshu's style of painting under the name Ze-an, made a small garden around the building Goko-no-ma in Reiun-in subtemple in the temple compound of Myoshin-ji. The central garden of Taizo-in subtemple, also of Myoshin-ji temple, is thought to be the work of Kano Motonobu (1475–1559), the master painter of the Kano school of painting, since there is a great amount of similarity between his painting style and the dry landscape garden and because he was related to one of the subtemples at Myoshin-ji.

Taizo-in (from *Miyako-Rinsen-Meisho-Zue*)

In summary, in the early days of this period large pond gardens were made for boating as at the villa of Gold Pavilion. Even the Silver Pavilion villa shows the influence of the garden style seen at Saiho-ji temple as well as the influence of the preceding age. In general, however, the *shinden* style of garden pond disappeared and the garden was used primarily for quiet strolling and meditation enjoyment. The dry landscape gardens could of course be used only for the pleasure gained in viewing them. They are like a painting, to be looked at and enjoyed, in that there were no paths upon which one could stroll.

Under the influence of the ordinary style of Zen priest residence houses, the *bukeshoin* style of architecture was developed. The garden, as well as buildings, underwent tremendous changes. The *shoin* of the *hojo* (living quarters of the priest) of Zen temples was the chief room of the residence where the chief priest of the temple spent the greater part of his time. Gardens connected to the living quarters were confined to a very narrow space; the most typical which made full use of this space is the dry landscape garden of Daisen-in temple. Originally the front yard of the living quarters was not turned into a garden but kept as a ground for important ceremonies. As the need for such ceremonies declined, the yard was made into a garden as was the case with the stone garden of Ryoan-ji temple. Such a garden compressed a large natural scene into a very narrow space by the use of high abstraction and profound symbolism. Thus the *kare-sansui* garden of the Muromachi period initiated a new style of garden into the history of the Japanese garden.

Momoyama Period (1573-1603)

The sixteenth century marked the end of the Japanese Middle Ages. The latter half of the Muromachi period, beginning with the Onin Civil War (1467-77), was a period of civil wars which lasted for a century up to the time of the unification of Japan by Oda Nobunaga (1534-82). He was followed by Toyotomi Hideyoshi (1536-98), and the gorgeous Momoyama period began. To describe briefly the Momoyama period we can say that it was an age in which man's ability was highly respected and recognized. The progressive policy and ambitiousness of Hideyoshi, who stood at the center of this period, was reflected in every aspect of the culture of this period and even in that which followed after his death.

The central characteristic of this period can be summed up by the word gorgeousness, which relates to Hideyoshi's ability and propensity to love anything pronounced. His love of gorgeous architecture gave birth to Osaka Castle and Jurakudai villa, and later reached a high point with the construction of

Fushimi Castle. Their gardens were likewise gorgeous and in keeping with the beauty of the architecture. All that remained of Jurakudai villa and Fushimi Castle of this period has been destroyed and there are no clues which might suggest what the original structure was like. Their splendor can be inferred well enough, however, from the buildings which were moved to Nishi Hongan-ji temple and other places. The visitor's hall of Nishi Hongan-ji, which is called Ko-no-ma (Hall of the Bean Goose), and its garden called Kokei-no-niwa (Garden of Tiger's Valley) are believed to have been moved from Fushimi Castle, while Hiunkaku (Hall of Flying Clouds) is the only remaining hall of Jurakudai.

Ko-no-ma of Nishi Hongan-ji

The general tendency of thought of this period which was led and unified by Hideyoshi was respect for the power of man rather than of God or of Buddha. Everything that existed was to serve man. This is illustrated, for example, in the Kokei-no-Niwa garden where a group of large rocks is set in the style Of a dry landscape garden, a style which ordinarily represented a great deal of religious symbolism. However, Hideyoshi used only the surface beauty of the stones without attempting to have them symbolize any religious feeling whatsoever, a fact which is illustrated by his use of a hewn stone bridge and many sago palms which had no religious symbolism and had not been seen in such gardens before.

Hideyoshi himself drew up the plans for the garden of Sanbo-in temple, and by using a number of workers brought it to a rough completion in a little over a month. His purpose was to complete it by spring and make it the center of a spring flower-viewing party. In August of the same year Hideyoshi suddenly died and it was not for another twenty years that the garden was actually completed, under the direction of Gien Jungo, chief priest of Sanbo-in temple. Looking at the building of the front hall (*omote-shoin*) the garden almost appears to be built in the *shinden* style of garden, arranged for boating and strolling, a type which became quite rare by the end of the Muromachi period. However, it actually is a *shoin*-style garden only for observation from the room. Hideyoshi's intention appears to have been to create a garden in which one could feel the atmosphere of court nobles and princes who enjoyed themselves in pond gardens. The two islands in the pond are connected by a bridge in spite of the fact that they represent the *horai* islands, crane island, and tortoise island respectively. Never before had these type of islands been connected by a bridge. Hideyoshi disregarded the convention and the prohibition which most traditional gardens observed. Although the traditional style of garden which was derived from Taoism and Buddhism was largely observed, Hideyoshi chose to vary the pattern and thus demonstrate clearly in the Sanbo-in garden the emphasis on the central place of man.

The garden of Nijo Castle is one of the best preserved of the castle gardens. It was initially made to serve as the residence of Ieyasu on his visits to Kyoto. The gorgeous hall of Ni-no-maru, the secondary citadel or fortress, reveals the tremendous power of the shogunate. In keeping with the splendor of the hall itself the garden pond with huge stones on the island and on the beach illustrates clearly the garden characteristics of this period to the fullest extent.

Although it is of the same period, Katsura Rikyu villa presents a quite different atmosphere of beauty from that of Nijo Castle. This was originally a suburban villa for the royal family designed and constructed by Prince Toshihito (1579–1629) and later enlarged and completed by his son, Prince Toshitada (1619–62). The harmonious beauty which exists between the houses and the garden is the product of the accomplishments and ability of these imperial princes and their collaborators. It is often contrasted with the beauty of Shugakuin Rikyu villa which was constructed by the retired emperor Gomizunoö (1596–1680) in the early Edo period, and a comparative study is interesting. Fundamentally, however, each has its own uniqueness and creates a quite different world. The garden of Katsura is a pond garden for both strolling about and for boating just as the large pond garden of the upper garden of Shugakuin. However, unlike Shugakuin, at Katsura the outside world is completely shut out, confining the view of the garden to the space within the walls surrounding it, without borrowing from the beauty of the distant hills and mountains. The buildings at Katsura were built for the enjoyment and daily living of the Imperial family and they included teahouses near the lake where refined taste could be enjoyed and expressed daily. Meticulous care is shown in the construction of the three main residential buildings and in the stone-paved paths which connect them. This is especially true of the paved stones which approach the front door. They are called Shin-no-shikiishi and their beauty is beyond description. The harmony between the buildings and the garden at Katsura Villa represents the ultimate in refined man-made beauty, an expression of beauty which will last forever.

Another noteworthy garden of this period is the garden of Honpo-ji temple at Teranouchi, Kamigyo section of Kyoto.

Shin-no-shikiishi of Katsura Rikyu

This is believed to be the only garden made by Hon'ami Koetsu. It is called Sanpa-no-niwa and is uniquely designed to symbolize the ideas of Nichiren (1222-82), who initiated the Nichiren sect of Buddhism. Dry landscape gardens, typical of this period, are also found in Juko-in subtemple within the Daitoku-ji compound and in Gyokuo-in subtemple within Myoshin-ji.

As we look to other districts in Japan, we find a small but typical *shoin* garden in Kojo-in within the compound of Onjo-ji temple in Otsu City and a large garden pond with an excellent stone arrangement and rock island in Genkyu-en garden at Hikone City. This latter type was the predecessor for mansion gardens which were made for feudal lords (*daimyo*). The Senshu-kaku garden within the castle of Tokushima is one of the earliest castle gardens built on a grand style in this period, and it has both a garden pond and a dry landscape garden. The gardens of Ni-no-maru and San-no-maru of Nagoya Castle are also splendid dry landscape gardens of this period.

Shoin and the garden of Kojo-in

It was in this period that the technique of trimming was developed and introduced into the garden, although trimming had also been seen in the background bushes of the dry waterfall in the garden of Daisen-in temple. The garden of Raikyu-ji temple in Takahashi City, in Okayama Prefecture, is thought to be the work of Kobori Enshu. It is regarded as the forerunner of the trimmed bush garden, for its main feature is found in the combination of trimmed bushes of various shapes. *Karikomi* trimming is the shaping of a bush or tree into an intended shape by trimming off and pruning away certain leaves and branches of a tree or bush. Trimming is always done with the intention of harmonizing the bush or tree with the arranged stones and building, and various methods are applied for this purpose.

It was also during this period that the teahouse garden, *roji,* was developed. This is a narrow garden along the approach to and around a teahouse. This was the result of the tea-ceremony vogue which had begun in the Higashiyama period and brought to perfection by Sen-no-Rikyu (1521–91). Instead of sumptuous tea parties, Rikyu was interested in *wabi-cha* (enjoyment of tea in quiet tasteful surroundings) and, as a result, the narrow teahouse garden called *roji* was developed. This represents the atmosphere of a lonely path leading to a mountain temple or that of a deep, tranquil valley.

Sen-no-Rikyu

Hideyoshi loved the tea ceremony and patronized Rikyu. The *wabi-cha* of Rikyu gained popularity among the *samurai* after the age of wars was over and during the time when such tea masters as Furuta Oribe and Hosokawa Sansai (or Tadaoki) appeared. Hon'ami Koetsu and Kobori Enshu, both disciples of the Oribe school of tea, developed the teahouse garden which subsequently became part of the tradition of the Japanese garden and their model was used and altered later in various ways. The ideals of the tea cult, *Sa-Zen-Ichimi* (Tea and Zen are one), and *Waki-Seijaku* (tranquil respect and serenity), are not only found in teahouse gardens but have been extended into the personalities and character of modern Japanese who respect the tea ceremony. These people look on these ideals as an accomplishment of Japanese character and enjoy and express them in their social circles.

It is from this period that stone lanterns and stone water-basins began to be widely used as points of interest and ornament without fulfilling their practical purposes. Although the teahouses and gardens which were made by Rikyu did not survive, they can be recalled by a visit to Tai-an teahouse of Myoki-an in Yamazaki and also in the garden approach to the teahouse on the ground of the Omote Senke family mansion. In various places throughout Japan one can find things which were favored, so they say, by Rikyu.

Edo Period (1603-1868)

The dominant mood of the Edo period was peaceful. In contrast to the Momoyama period, which was at once gorgeous as well as powerful, this period fell into a condition of triviality and became worse toward the end. However, in the early era of this period many excellent gardens were constructed.

The best garden architect of the early Edo period was Kobori Enshu, who had begun designing and creating gardens in the Momoyama period. His finest gardens were built during the twenty years of the Kan'ei era (1624-44, a subperiod within the Edo period), the time of his mature years beginning when he was in his fifties.

Among the gardens which Enshu designed there is the Nino-maru garden of Nijo Castle, to which reference has been made above. In 1626 for the Emperor Gomizunoö's visit to the castle, Enshu constructed the garden as a focal point of beauty outside of the hall where the Emperor was to stay. In the following year he became the director for the construction of Sento Gosho (the palace of the retired emperor, or *Joko*) for Gomizunoö. The gardens he constructed at this time were the northern garden of Nyoin Gosho for Tofukumon'in and the southern garden of Sento Gosho. These two gardens still

North Garden of Sento Gosho

Gonai-tei of Kyoto Gosho

exist at Sento Gosho, which occupies an area at the southeast corner of the large compound of Kyoto Imperial Palace. The ground near the lake of the southern garden is covered by rounded flat stones called Odawara-Ishi and represents a view of the seashore in miniature. The view of the garden is grand as is true of the pond garden called Oike-niwa at Kyoto Imperial Palace. The imposing stones on the peninsula and the beach reveal the fine technique of Enshu.

In 1640 Enshu directed the construction of Kyoto Imperial Palace and he built the pond garden in front of Kogosho hall (p. 42). This beach is also covered with rounded flat stones, and a bridge connects the island to the land. It is in good harmony with the large nearby halls and is full of dignity.

Related to the temple gardens designed by Enshu, one should mention Konchi-in, one of the subtemples of Nanzen-ji temple (p. 21). Suden, who was highly trusted by Ieyasu, asked Enshu to design the garden, and Kentei and other garden architects made the garden following Enshu's layout. Beyond the stretch of white sand lie two stone islands, crane and tortoise islands, with gravel spread over the ground between them, and other stone islands are also in evidence. The mound in the background is covered with large trimmed bushes. A large prayer stone faces toward the Tosho-gu shrine, the mausoleum of Ieyasu, and the garden is a typical crane-tortoise garden in which the prosperity of the Tokugawa family was prayed for.

The large abbot's residence of Nanzen-ji temple was once the Seiryo-den hall of the Imperial Palace. The garden over which the *hojo* looks (p. 20) was also made by Enshu at Suden's request. This garden helps to create a very dignified residence for the chief abbot, but it is short of Enshu's highest masterpieces, perhaps for the reason that the garden was added at a later time.

By far the most important work of Kobori Enshu is Kohoan temple within the compound of Daitoku-ji. This was originally built in Ryuko-in temple by Enshu as a temple to pray for the repose of his ancestor's souls, but it was moved in 1643 to the present site when Enshu was sixty-five years old in order that he might spend the remaining years of his life at the temple in easy retirement after having won fame and a lasting name. The powerful structure of the stone bridge in front of the front gate (p. 47) shows without reserve his genius. The most charming feature of Koho-an is Bosen-seki teahouse and the small *roji* garden it overlooks. Enshu's originality and re-

Roji of Bosen-seki in Koho-an

fined technique is observed in the unrivaled design of the *shoji* (paper sliding doors) which run on a beam installed halfway between the ceiling and the floor. The upper half of the garden is thus blocked from view by the sliding doors enabling only the lower half to be seen. This idea, it is believed, was taken from the window of a Japanese ship. Also worthy of note at Koho-an are the fore garden, Jikinyu-ken, the teahouse called San'unjo, and the garden surrounding and approaching it as well as the stone water basins and the stone lanterns found there.

There are some other gardens believed to have been made by Enshu: the east garden of the main temple of Daitoku-ji, and the garden of Shoden-ji temple at Nishi-Gamo with only trimmed bushes and sand (p. 35). The garden of large trimmed bushes at Daichi-ji temple (p. 82) in Mizuguchi-cho, Shiga, is thought to have been made by Enshu in honor of the lord who had appointed him to be the director of repairs at Mizuguchi Castle. Compared with the garden of Raikyu-ji temple in Takahashi City in Okayama Prefecture, this garden is small in scale, but it has been made with the same technique.

Dry landscape gardens of the early Edo period are found at the following temples: the abbot's residence of the main temple of Daitoku-ji, the abbot's residence of Suon-an temple (called also Takigi-Ikkyu-ji), the large and small guest houses of Manshu-in temple at Ichijo-ji, Sanzen-in temple at Ohara, (first constructed in the Heian period), Entsu-ji temple at Hataeda, and Obai-in temple within the compound of Daitoku-ji. With the exception of the gardens at Manshu-in and Sanzen-in which are temples related to the Tendai sect of Buddhism, all of the others are Zen temple gardens. Pond gardens of this period are those at Joju-in temple in the main temple of Kiyomizu-dera and at such temples as Chishaku-in, Shoren-in, Kodai-ji, Renge-ji near Yase and Ninna-ji of Omuro. Gardens of rather unique style are found at Shisen-do villa made by Ishikawa Jozan and the garden of Kaisan-do hall, at Tofuku-ji, which is a combination pond garden and dry landscape garden. There are many other gardens of this period which are found in Kyoto including Rinkyu-ji temple which had as the chief priest a princess of the Imperial family, and Reikan-ji temple, and the teahouse garden of the Ura Senke family and the *roji* garden of the Yabunouchi family. Finally the garden of Shugakuin Imperial Villa must be mentioned as also an Edo garden. These important gardens will be discussed in more detail later.

As we look to the other districts of Japan we find that pond gardens and the combination of pond garden characteristics with dry landscape elements are found in Enman-in temple of Otsu, Kongorin-ji, Saimyo-ji, Fukuju-ji, and Ryotan-ji temples to the east of Lake Biwa. Dry landscape gardens are found at Rakuraku-en garden in Hikone, and at Seigan-ji temple in Maibara. In Sakamoto there is a pond garden at Shiga-in temple and Ritsu-in temple has a garden which features a running stream. In Nara there are two lovely gardens: the garden of Jiko-ji temple presents a unique view with a number of beautifully trimmed trees, and the pond garden of Hokke-ji temple is also charming.

The most remarkable characteristic of this period is the *daimyo* gardens which were made in the castle towns of large feudal domains. In Edo, the capital of the Tokugawa government, a large garden with ponds was made in Edo Castle by Kobori Enshu and many other gardens were built at the resident mansions of numerous *daimyo* for their enjoyment when they were staying in the capital. Among the surviving gardens of this kind, the most famous found in Tokyo are Koraku-en which belonged to the Mito family, Hama Rikyu (villa) which first belonged to the Tokugawa family and later became imperial property, and Rikugi-en garden of the Yanagisawa family. Famous gardens in other areas of Japan are Ritsurin Park in Takamatsu City, Koraku-en garden in Okayama, Suizenji Seishu-en garden in Kumamoto, Kairaku-en garden in Mito, and Kenroku-en garden in Kanazawa, which was built in the mid-Edo period. In the days when the feudal system was firmly established and the times seemed to show promise of a peaceful age to come, the strong *daimyo* who owned large domains enlarged their castles and constructed large gardens, many of which were large pond gardens for strolling, while others were designed for both strolling and boating.

In this way the gardens of the early Edo period retained some characteristics of the Momoyama period, while at the same time they reflected the spirit of the *samurai* who fought hard in many battles, that is, the gardens were energetic and unique. By the middle of the period, however, the garden was becoming smaller in scale and eventually descended to an even trivial technique. This was largely the result of the general trend of the times in which the mode of living became gaudy. It was at this time that the *samurai* class began to have fewer battles to fight and they led largely idle lives, while at the same time nobles only maintained their appearance precariously since the culture of the common people was becoming more and more prosperous. This trend became fatal to the quality of the culture as time went on.

There are only a few gardens of this later period which are worth noticing: Hoshun-in, Koto-in and Obai-in, subtemples of the Daitoku-ji compound, and Keishun-in of the Myoshin-ji compound and the garden of the study hall of Ryosoku-in within the compound of Ken'nin-ji temple. Also included in this book are the temple gardens of Jisso-in (for which the data of construction is not known), Jakko-in, Konpuku-ji, and the unique garden of Honen-in temple. Gardens whose point of interest lie more in the natural surroundings than in the gardens themselves are those of Kozan-ji, Koetsu-ji, and Joshoko-ji temples. Of particular interest is the *tsubo-niwa* (miniature garden) of Tokai-an within the compound of Myoshin-ji temple, where one finds carefully set in a small garden of raked white sand seven rocks of various size producing a most exquisite atmosphere. This garden was made in 1814 by a Buddhist bonze, Toboku.

Throughout Japan there are many gardens which were made in this later Edo period, but only a few of exceptional quality. From Shiga Prefecture only the gardens of Daitsu-ji temple in Nagahama and Gesshin-ji temple, Otsu City, are included. From the Tohoku district we have included the gardens of the Honma Art Museum in Sakata City and of the Chido Museum which belongs to the Sakai family in Tsuruoka City. I would also like to mention the unique rock garden of Tsukinokatsura found in the mansion of Katsura, a former minister of the Mori clan, located in Bofu City in Yamaguchi Prefecture (p. 102).

A word should be added regarding the large pond gardens which were built in the mansions of important *daimyo*. These gardens were modeled after the traditional *horai* gardens which included the crane and tortoise islands derived from Taoism and were placed in the garden for the prosperity and longevity of each member of the family. The real spirit and faith in Taoism, however, had gradually vanished and the inclusion of these elements in the garden was more an imitation of technique than a regard for its religious meaning. The same can largely be said in regard to the dry landscape gardens.

We also find throughout the entire Edo period the development of the teahouse. In the gardens of the *daimyo* mentioned above and others, many teahouses were constructed. In the teahouse gardens beautiful stone lanterns and water basins were aesthetically placed, and one also began to find the extensive use of lovely stepping stones leading to the teahouses. These tea gardens became the pattern for the ordinary gardens

Tsubo-niwa of
Tokai-an

which many Japanese now have adjoining their houses.

From the Meiji Period to the Present (1868–   )

The Meiji Restoration marked the dawn of modern Japan. The colorful innovations in the political and social sphere and in economics and international relations were numerous. With the development of thought, learning, and science, traditional Japanese thought largely came to be disregarded.

In such an age, the minds of the people were hardly directed to the field of either new or old art, to say nothing of the garden. It was only in the tenth year of the Emperor Meiji (1878) that a faint sign of encouragement toward art began to be seen, and only after the Sino-Japanese War of 1894–95 did the encouragement become earnest. Prior to this, Tokyo and other cities had been provided with parks, greatly different from Japanese gardens, which had been modeled after European parks. Some of the *daimyo* gardens underwent remodeling at this time and were turned into public parks open to visitors. In the same way, many Western-style buildings were constructed and their gardens became either Westernized or an amalgamation of Western and Japanese styles. This trend continued on through the Taisho era.

Since the tradition of Japanese gardens was felt so very strong in Kyoto and due in part to the high quality of natural scenery in and around the city, Kyoto was fortunately not greatly affected by this trend toward Westernization. Thus there was little room for the Western style of garden. After the victory of the Sino-Japanese War many millionaires as well as peers constructed villas in the area of Nanzen-ji and Okazaki in Kyoto. Murin-an villa, belonging to Yamagata Aritomo (1838–1922), is one of the earliest gardens of this kind and one of the finest naturalistic gardens that was constructed. At about the same time the construction of a large pond garden was begun (in the 28th year of the Emperor Meiji, 1895) within the grounds of Heian Shrine. This was completed in the early Taisho era.

A common characteristic of these gardens was the use of the *shakkei* technique, that is the borrowing of the distant view of Higashiyama mountains as their background as if by common consent, and a similar style of construction by including a pond, waterfall, and stream, making use of the overflowing drainage water from Lake Biwa's reservoir which had been constructed at that time. Their architect was Ogawa Jihei whose professional name was Ueji (d. 1932), a most skilled garden architect who carried out the intention of the owner

South Garden of Hojo of
Tofuku-ji

Kare-sansui garden of
Rakusui-en

Kare-sansui garden of
Kaisan-do

and his own preference, to imitate nature. As a result, though different in layout, the gardens presented similar characteristics. Murin-an villa is perhaps the most representative of them all (p. 22). It reflects the intention of Yamagata Aritomo, who as a soldier loved *waka* (a 31-syllable Japanese poem) and possessed elegant taste.

The gardens of Heian Shrine including the West, the Central, and the East gardens were made by Ogawa Jihei. The East garden is the latest and the largest (p. 18). With various carefully arranged plants and flowers it presents a beautiful sight in keeping with the magnificent buildings of the shrine.

Pioneering work in new garden construction is found in the abbot's residence of Tofuku-ji temple which was built in 1938 by Shigemori Mirei. He also constructed the gardens of Komyo-in within Tofuku-ji and Zuiho-in within the compound of Daitoku-ji temple, as well as others in Kyoto, the Chugoku, San'in, and Shikoku districts. The total number of gardens which he has built for temples or private homes numbers more than one hundred and fifty. Nakane Kinsaku, besides engaging in garden research and repair of old gardens, has constructed Rakusui-en garden of Jonangu and the garden of Goko-no-miya shrine and the southern garden of Taizo-in temple. In addition to these two there are many other garden specialists and garden architects who have constructed an increasing number of different style gardens for public gardens as well as for private homes. These gardens are far advanced in technique and beauty to the gardens of Ogawa Jihei. For the most part these newer gardens are directed toward the tradition of dry landscape garden and, to our great interest, toward a new creative work.

COMMENTARY ON THE GARDENS

Reference to the gardens is made in the order of their appearance in the picture section, but omitted is the reference to the gardens which have already been alluded to in "The History of Japanese Gardens."

Eastern Kyoto

The garden of Kaisan-do hall (p. 10) is the garden in front of the founder's hall Joraku-an, on the eastern side of the large temple grounds of Tofuku-ji. On one side there is a dry landscape garden built according to the *horai* style of garden with crane and tortoise islands on the white stretch of sand, together with a few small, neatly trimmed bushes and trees. Because of the profound stillness and quietude here, it is considered to be the holiest area of the temple.

The *hojo* of Tofuku-ji was reconstructed during the Meiji era and Shigemori Mirei was responsible for the construction of the gardens surrounding it in 1938 (p. 11). The main garden lies to the south of the temple and represents the ideal world of Taoism.

The gardens of Funda-in temple, which are believed to have been constructed originally by Sesshu, were also reconstructed by Shigemori (p. 12). The East Garden reminds one of a small picture painted by Sesshu. The garden of Komyo-in temple (p. 13), also within the Tofuku-ji compound, was also constructed by Shigemori Mirei in 1939. Its name, which means the heart of the wave, is taken from a phrase of Zen Buddhism. This garden is the best of the gardens made by Shigemori, certainly holding the interest of the visitor and deserving its recognition as a new garden of special merit. In more recent years Shigemori has constructed a garden for the abbot's residence of Ryugen-an temple which is the oldest structure of this temple.

The lovely temple, Chishaku-in at Higashiyama-Shichijo, Kyoto (p. 14), whose predecessor was Shoun-ji temple, is the burial ground of Hideyoshi's eldest son, Tsurumatsu. It is a member temple of the Chizan branch of the Shingon sect of Buddhism. Although the pond is quite narrow, the garden is sequestered and quiet. The scene, which includes a miniature mound, a dry waterfall, and a stone bridge, is splendid to behold. Looking at the garden from the north, an entirely different perspective and beauty confronts the eye, due merely to the change of perspective. The pictures which are painted on the sliding screen doors, or *fusuma*, are first-rate National Treasures which were formerly found in Shoun-ji temple.

The garden of Joju-in, the central hall of Kiyomizu-dera temple (p. 15), has long been considered as an excellent garden. A stone lantern, which stands at the foot of a small mound on the other side of Yuya-dani (a small valley) is an extremely impressive focal point of the garden. The whole garden certainly expresses the beauty of artistic refinement.

At Shoren-in temple (p. 17) a garden path leads around the pond to the garden which is called Kirishima-no-Niwa and a teahouse, Kobuntei. Even so the garden's primary function is not for strolling but for quiet observation from the building. Near the gate there are impressive and aged camphor trees.

The environment and mood of Honen-in temple (p. 23) is

The East Garden of Fundain.

Pictures of cherry trees and maple trees on the fusuma of Chishaku-in

Joju-in (from *Chikuzan-Teizo-Den*)

very attractive. This temple was originally built by Banbu of Chion-in temple toward the end of the early Edo period. The temple is closely related to Japanese *haiku* poetry, since the priest of this temple is the poet-priest Nyoze. In the graveyard of the temple one finds numerous tombs of literary men and scholars.

Hakusa-sonso villa (p. 25) has, like Entoku-in temple, only been recently open to the public. It was formerly the villa garden of the late painter Hashimoto Kansetsu. In a posthumous manuscript discovered after his death, it was found that the garden was built to realize in his words that, "to make a garden and paint a picture are one and the same thing." With his large studio at the center, the garden includes the following five features: the pond, two teahouses, Isui-tei and Sui-tei, lovely *sawatari* (stepping stones in the pond), and a stone bridge. The white pine tree in front of the Jibutsu-do, a small Buddhist chapel, is a rare species of Chinese pine. Also wonderful is the wide variety of collected stoneworks from the Heian, Kamakura, and Muromachi periods. In short this is a garden which only Kansetsu could have made. The garden is permeated with an acute sense of beauty which only a master artist could create.

The last garden in the eastern Kyoto section is that of Jisho-ji temple (p. 24), where one finds the Silver Pavilion and Togu-do hall. Of great interest is the man Yoshimasa and the colorful days known as the Higashiyama period. Here was a man who disregarded governmental politics and the Onin Civil War and instead indulged himself in an appreciation of art and beauty with elegant taste. Living in the midst of such troubled times, no wonder he is so bitterly criticized. However he could do nothing other than what he did. He felt deeply the transiency of the world and he loved the garden as he loved nature in its natural surroundings. In addition, one can say that Yoshimasa lived a life in pursuit of truth.

The Higashiyama-den villa was turned into a temple with a name of Jisho-ji after his death. Soon after, the process of dilapidation began and shortly afterward the ground became a battlefield. With the exception of the Silver Pavilion and Togu-do hall, all the buildings were destroyed and the garden was laid to waste. Repair was not begun until the early Edo period when Miyagi Toyomori began the task which was continued by his son and grandson. The Miyagi family thus also felt a strong attachment to the villa. Interestingly in the vicissitudes of Higashiyama-den villa one appears to see the evanescent quality of man's labors. However, the Higashiyama culture

Ginkaku-ji (from *Miyako-Rinsen-Meisho-Zue*)

which Yoshimasa and the skillful artists around him established, later blossomed into full flower, until today it occupies an imperishable place in the history of arts and crafts. Though the garden has changed over the years, it still has a highly historical and artistic value.

An especially noteworthy scene in the garden is that which lies in front of the Togu-do hall, this being a portion of the original garden which included the island and stone bridge. If one ignores the actual date of construction and the historical facts, it is possible to see in the composition of a mound of sand (Ginsa-dan) and a sand work (Kogetsu-dai) what almost appears to be modern abstract art.

Near the passage from the abbot's residence to Togu-do hall there is a small garden with a stone water basin, which is called the Ginkaku-ji style of basin, and a stone lantern. Such a small garden called *tsubo-niwa* is often found in temples and is often a model for gardens built for private houses.

The garden was undoubtedly designed and the construction supervised by Yoshimasa. In addition there was a director for construction, a chief worker, and numerous other ordinary workers. Zen'ami, a *senzui-kawaramono* (special class of people at that time who were specially trained to work as the garden director ordered), was the chief worker, and he and his son Koshiro and his grandson Matashiro played important roles.

Northern Kyoto

Shisen-do is the hermitage where Ishikawa Jozan (1583–1672) spent his retirement (p. 26). Both the house and the garden were built by him. Due to his profound knowledge and scholarship as a scholar of Confucianism and Neo-Confucianism, the house and garden were built in a Chinese style. The beautiful shape of the trimmed bushes and the long stretch of white sand, which you look out upon, present a beautiful scene. In the autumn season of maple leaves it will be as beautiful, as we say in Japanese, as the twilled brocade and fallen petals of a large sasanqua float reflected on the sand. The quiet sound of the *sozu-kakehi* (bamboo water device which makes a clacking sound) can be heard nearby. The *sozu-kakehi* here is quite original and matches its surroundings. Such an impression is given by the garden. Although it was built in a Chinese style, it still remains essentially a Japanese garden which incorporates basic Chinese elements. The front garden is a dry landscape garden but in the eastern corner there is a tiny waterfall and the water runs near the outer porch of the building. Among the trimmed bushes there is a small stone pagoda and the

Ginkaku-ji style stone water basin

Sozu at Shisen-do

garden stretches along to the east of the study room. After looking down at the garden from the inside of the house, step down into the garden itself and notice the strange appearance of the Shogetsu-ro hall.

Konpuku-ji temple is not far from Shisen-do. The garden (p. 27) of this temple is beautiful in its natural simplicity with only a white stretch of sand and trimmed azalea bushes.

Manshu-in temple (p. 28) is a *monzeki* temple, that is, a temple whose chief priest is an Imperial Prince. In the profound quietude of its location at Nishi-Sakamoto at the foot of Mt. Hiei it presents the dignified aspect of a mountain temple. The garden lies to the south of the two neat small and large study halls. The son of Hachijo-no-miya, the priest-prince Ryosho, who constructed Katsura Imperial Villa, designed the buildings and the garden with true genius. The picture of the garden on page 28 was taken from the inside of the study hall. The transom above is decorated with a design of chrysanthemum flowers. In the garden there is a standing stone which suggests a waterfall—an excellent idea—and the crane and tortoise islands floating on the stream of white sand are indeed noble. Fukuro (owl)-no-chozubachi, the stone water basin in front of the smaller study hall, is not for practical use, but instead has symbolic significance. The base represents the tortoise and the sculpture on the basin itself is believed to represent the crane

Fukuro-no-chozubachi at Manshu-in

Rinkyu-ji temple (p. 29) is found within the grounds of Shugakuin Imperial Villa. The small pond garden beside the temple has a feminine quality which reflects the elegance of the first priest-princess who built the garden, Fumyoin-Shozan-Genyo-ni. On the low hill which adjoins the garden there is the founder's hall where she is enshrined. The wooden image of this first priest-princess is beautiful, and the elegant Boran-tei arbor and Higaki-no-to pagoda are splendid.

Shugakuin Imperial Villa is often compared with Katsura Imperial Villa. However, each has its own individual characteristics. Shugakuin was constructed by the retired emperor Gomizunoö and was called a *sanso* (mountain villa) or *ochaya* (literally, teahouse). In 1884 the Imperial Household Agency took it over and it became an Imperial villa.

This villa's construction was begun in 1656 and completed in three years. The villa's main attraction is the upper garden called Kami-no-Ochaya while the house in the lower garden, Shimo-no-Ochaya, served as a kind of resthouse for the Emperor on his visits. The house of the middle garden called Naka-no-Ochaya was built at a later data as a gift to the Princess Teruko for her to use as a residence and called Akeno-miya Palace. This building later became the Rinkyu-ji temple, to which reference was made above.

The consort of the Emperor Gomizunoö, Kazuko, was the daughter of Hidetada, the second shogun of the Tokugawa clan, and she called herself Tofukumon'in after the Emperor's abdication.

The main attraction of the upper garden, Kami-no-Ochaya, is the lovely pond Yokuryu-chi (p. 30). The pond is fed from the dam on the Otowa River and the large bank of the pond, which was built with four layers of stone walls, stretches with the large trimmed bushes growing on it along Nishihama beach. The grand view from Rin'un-tei hall, for which the villa was primarily constructed, has a matchless magnificence, in spite of the fact that the garden was built in the style which borrowed from distant views. Anyone who once stands at Rin'un-tei looking out over the pond and the scene beyond, will utter a cry of wonder and admiration. It is claimed by some that the garden represents superhuman achievement and it is admired as an example of Japanese thinking about the composition of the world at that time. The historical record indicates that the design of every tree and stone was drawn up by Gomizunoö himself but the actual construction was conducted under the supervision of Hiramatsu Kashin, a favorite gardener of the Emperor.

After the Second World War, visitors have been allowed to visit this villa and that at Katsura by appointment and the permission of the Imperial Household Agency at designated periods. Both gardens leave one with a deep impression of beauty, for it is believed that a thing of excellence is always original, forever fresh, and eternally filled with modern sensibility.

The architecture found at the villa is rather plain but an incomparable gracefulness is found near the west window of Kyusui-tei arbor and in the organization of Jodan-no-ma room. The main attraction of the lower garden, Shimo-no-Ochaya, is Jugetsukan arbor and its garden (p. 31). Although the stepping stones are lovely, the garden to the south of the running stream has been altered, it is believed, from its original design. At one time there was a hall called Wankyoku-kaku from which Gomizunoö would watch the farmers laboring in the fields nearby. The field to the south of the garden has been retained as an agricultural field and it too presents a lovely sight as each season passes on. The paths within the garden, which are lined with pine trees, Mt. Shugakuin to the east of Kami-

Kasumi-dana of the guest hall

no-Ochaya, and Mt. Hiei which stands nobly behind and above the others, are also beautiful.

Rakushiken arbor at Naka-no-Ochaya survives from the days of Akenomiya Palace and the guest hall was once the interviewing hall of Tofukumon'in, the name Kazuko took after her husband's abdication. Quite different from the other buildings, these halls are decorated in great splendor according to the preference of the fine lady who resided here. In this respect one may note the shelves or Kasumi-dana which are seen in the marginal picture. But in contrast to this splendor of the architecture, the garden with sequestered and quiet atmosphere is worth appreciating to our heart's content.

At Jakko-in temple (p. 32) the pathetic story of Kenrei-mon'in which is related in the *Heike Monogatari* (The Tales of the Heike Clan), upon recollection, gives a special atmosphere to the scene around the small garden, the central hall, and her statue enshrined within the inner hall. Nagisa-no-Ike pond and the small pond and waterfall to the south of the central hall enhance the pathetic atmosphere of this temple.

In Sanzen-in temple at Ohara (p. 33) there are two main gardens. One is the moss garden along the path to and around Ojo-Gokuraku-in hall, in which three Amida Buddhist images are enshrined. This garden, of which much has been spoken in recent years, is called Ruriko-tei, and it is known for its beautiful quietude (*jaku*) and the subtle play of light (*ko*) which is found there. A small area called Yusei-en occupies a corner within this garden and has a pond called the pond of the Eight Mercies of Paradise (Hachi-Kudoku-Ike) in which a tortoise island is found. Because of the tall cedar and maple trees in Ruriko-tei garden, the garden presents a sequestered aspect quite in harmony with one's frame of mind when praying to the Amitabha. The other garden is Shuheki-en to the south of the guest hall. The clear pond beautifully reflects the sunlight and the trees which surround it. Looking at Ojo-Gokuraku-in hall from the veranda of the guest hall also gives one an indescribably beautiful picture. It is believed that both gardens were made by the priest Shiba in the late Heian period and then later remodeled by Kanamori Sowa, a *daimyo* and master of the tea ceremony living in the early Edo period.

Entsu-ji temple (p. 34) was once Hataeda Villa, or Hataeda-no-Ochaya, before Gomizunoö built Shugakuin Villa. Here, the Emperor Reigen spent his early days and his nurse, Ben'ei-ni, later turned the villa into a Zen temple. As the picture on the left shows, there were buildings of the villa on top of the hill and at its foot. The borrowed background beauty of Mt.

Entsu-ji (from *Supplement to Miyako-Meisho-Zue*)

Hiei convinces us that the theory that this holy mountain stood for Buddha is correct.

Shoden-ji temple (p. 35) is located near Mt. Myoken, the site of an annual bonfire which is lit for the souls of the dead at Obon in the middle of July in Kyoto, and forms the shape of a ship. The temple was reconstructed by a Zen priest, Kokaku, who prayed for the victory of Japan during the Yuan invasion in the thirteenth century. The building for the abbot's residence is that of a hall which was moved from Fushimi Castle, and the pictures on the sliding screen doors were painted by Kano Sanraku. The composition of the garden includes only trimmed bushes in sizes in the ratio of seven, five and three.

Renge-ji temple (p. 35) is near the Takano River in the area of Miyakehachiman. The temple was reconstructed by Imaeda Minbu, an old subject of the Maeda clan in the province of Kaga, and it belongs to the Tendai sect. The pond garden is a *horai* paradise garden with the two islands representing the crane and the tortoise. The feretory in the central hall and the lantern, the prototype of the Renge-ji style of lantern, are worthy of note.

The central attraction of Koetsu-ji temple (p. 37) is the area around Taikoan teahouse. Further charm is added with the beauty of the three mountains of Takagamine. It is from such natural beauty that the artistic work and creation of Hon'ami Koetsu (1558-1634, calligrapher, painter, ceramist, lacquerwork artist, and master of tea ceremony) were born.

Central Kyoto

The garden called Kokei-no-niwa (p. 38) of Nishi Hongan-ji temple looks small against the gorgeous magnificence of Taimensho hall which is so wide that 203 *tatami* (straw mat flooring, each mat approximately 1 m. × 2 m.) are used in the room. Nevertheless the garden yields little even when compared to the splendor of Taimensho hall. The central feature of the garden is the stones which have been used to form the dry waterfall in the *sanson* style of stone arrangement and the bridge of hewn stone in front of the waterfall. Cycad or sago palm trees, which give a South Seas atmosphere to the garden, enhance the artistic effect.

There is another garden at Nishi Hongan-ji temple called Tekisui-en (p. 39) in front of Hiunkaku hall. The only remaining building of Hideyoshi's villa, Jurakudai, this Hiunkaku hall dates back to the Momoyama period and interests us mostly as a clue to imagine the splendor and gorgeousness of the now lost Jurakudai Villa. The Tekisuien garden was built after Hiunkaku hall was moved from Jurakudai, and the garden is thus the loser when compared to the splendor of Hiunkaku hall.

A teahouse cannot exist without a *roji,* or teahouse garden. The *roji* garden's primary purpose of course is to be a path which will lead one to the teahouse, but at the same time it serves as a beautiful scene in and of itself. According to a great master of tea ceremony, Rikyu: "Stepping stones are sixty percent practical and forty percent a thing of beauty." These were his words concerning the ratio of the practical and the beautiful in regard to the stepping stones, however, they are not referring only to the stepping stones but to the whole *roji.*

The *roji* garden of the hut style in Rikyu's *wabi-cha* was originally a plain single garden, but in the course of time, double and triple gardens were made according to the number of gates separating one section from another, and also a *roji* garden in the *shoin* style. If the teahouse was located in a large garden an appropriately sized *roji* was of course built.

The gate to the teahouse of the Omote Senke family (p. 44), which was called the *nakakuguri,* marks the boundary between the outer *roji* and the inner *roji.* In the days of Rikyu there was only a single *roji,* however, so the gate was a simple wicket, which was given the name *nakakuguri* by Oribe and was called *chumon* by Enshu. When a tea ceremony is held, the host comes to meet the guests at this gate and from here they proceed into the inner *roji* stopping before entering the teahouse to rinse their mouths and wash their hands with the water running into the stone water basin, that is, *tsukubai,* standing near the teahouse. The gate of this garden is typical of this particular style and serves in addition to marking the boundary as an effective way of narrowing the view, giving a deeper appearance to the inner garden. In the outer *roji* garden, to add a parenthesis, one finds only such things as the waiting room, a bench, and toilet.

The chief feature of the house of the Omote Senke family is the building Fushin-an and that of the Ura Senke family, the building, Konnichi-an. The picture that has been included from the Ura Senke garden is the stone-paved approach (p. 45) behind the Kabuto-mon gate. Konnichi-an is a teahouse devoted solely to the spirit of simplicity and its *roji* garden is in perfect harmony with it. Interestingly one of the teahouses is a modern one without *tatami,* appropriate for the spirit of a new age.

Turning to Daitoku-ji temple we find a fine example of dry landscape garden in the south garden of the abbot's residence

Roji of Fushin-an

in the central temple (p. 46). There is a particularly wide stretch of raked white sand with a set of large rocks forming a dry waterfall beneath a carefully pruned tree in the southeast corner. From these rocks there are others which lead off to the west along the earthen wall. The white stretch of sand stands for the sea. A rock near the outer porch serves as the point of unity for the rocks, trees, and sand in the garden. The rocks of the dry waterfall are not particularly magnificent nor overbearing, but rather they are composed. That is to say, there is the implication that the rocks of the dry landscape gardens in Zen temples do not always give an impression of severity or rigidity. It is believed that the east garden was made by Enshu and formerly borrowed from the distant view of Mt. Hiei.

In the rear of the abbot's residence of the central temple one finds the temple called Shinju-an where Ikkyu Sojun lived. During the Onin Civil War the compound of Daitoku-ji temple was almost completely burned down. Ikkyu devoted himself to the reconstruction of other temples leaving his own temple behind. After his death a wealthy merchant of Sakai, Owa Sorin, reconstructed Shinju-an as he had promised to Ikkyu. The east garden is like that of the central temple and has rocks in the ratio of seven, five, and three (p. 46).

Many of the subtemples of Daitoku-ji, such as Shinju-an, Koho-an, Juko-in, as well as the central temple, are not open to the public. Daisen-in was the first subtemple of the Daitoku-ji compound to open its doors to the public. This is of great significance, for the dry landscape garden of Daisen-in marks, together with that at Ryoan-ji temple, the zenith of the Muromachi period. The garden of Daisen-in (p. 48) is located to the northeast of the abbot's residence which has been designated as an official National Treasure. Within the narrow space of about 100 square meters, there are rocks and stones of various shapes and sizes which represent a landscape of steep mountains and deep valleys. The marvelous symbolism and creativity of this garden lies beyond the capacity of words to express its exquisiteness.

This garden is divided into two parts by a stone bridge called Teikyo or Kyoro. In 1961 after the garden was dismantled for repair it was reconstructed again according to an old picture. Different reasons have been given for its existence and some question whether or not it should be there at all. At any rate the decisive composition of the bridge gives a more profound depth to the garden and makes us aware of the elaborate harmony of the whole. Since there is no doubt about the

Stepping stones of
Shinju-an

sensitive harmony between the garden and the building the unmistakable conclusion seems to be that the stone bridge was placed here not for convenience sake but for the sake of the artistic proportion of the garden.

The south garden of this temple is a single stretch of white sand. The garden of white sand which is found at many Zen temples is a very old style usually associated with the front gardens of the abbot's residence of Zen temples. At this temple the stretch of white sand represents the ocean with the dry stream from the northeast garden flowing into it. This is best kept in mind when viewing the garden.

The *shoin* hall to the north of the abbot's residence is believed to have been the residence of the famous priest Takuan (1573 –1645). In front of this there is a rock garden. Even though it was made rather recently, it has an atmosphere of profound quietude.

A portion of the south garden of the abbot's residence at Hoshun-in subtemple is a charming garden of Chinese balloon flowers (p. 49). Just when the flowers were first planted is not known. However, the flowers remind one of the beautiful and chaste Hoshun-in who was a helpful partner of Maeda Toshiie.

The main garden of Hoshun-in temple is the garden to the north of the abbot's residence. The picture in the margin is from the *Miyako-Rinsen-Meisho-Zue* (Pictures of Famous Scenic Gardens of Kyoto). This garden is a landscape garden with buildings and at its center is the tower Donko-kaku, in which are enshrined the images of Sugawara Michizane, an ancestor of the Maeda family, and Gyokushitsu, the first priest of the temple. Visitors are not allowed to enter this building but the gracious figure of Mt. Hiei as seen from the second floor is perhaps equal to, if not the best view in all of Kyoto. The sleeping lotuses in the pond and the various flowers on the beach are also reminiscent of the taste of the noble Hoshun-in.

Hoshun-in (from *Miyako-Rinsen-Meisho-Zue*)

Koto-in subtemple was constructed as an offering for the peace of Hosokawa Yusai's soul by his son Tadaoki (or Sansai), who was like one of the seven philosophical masters of tea, a typical war lord well versed in the exquisite lore of Zen. The study hall to the north of the guest house is thought to have been moved from the house of Rikyu which was located at Ebiya-cho, Ichijo in Kyoto. The stone lantern which now serves as the tombstone over the grave of Sansai and his wife Gracia, is a superb work of art which was treasured by Rikyu, who, according to a legend, in order to refuse Hideyoshi's desire for it, damaged it slightly and gave it to Sansai.

The large water basin in the *roji* garden (p. 50) as seen from the teahouse, Horai, which lies to the northwest of the guest house, was formerly a foundation stone of a Korean castle, and was brought back from a Korean expedition (1592–98). It is quite imposing and is said to represent the *kesa* style of water basin. In the fall, the south garden of the guest house is colored by the crimson leaves of the Japanese maple trees, so much so that the hall itself is colored a beautiful crimson with the reflection and even the visitors' faces themselves take on the gorgeous crimson hue.

Obai-in, another subtemple, was designed and constructed by Kobayakawa Takakage. One half of the south garden of the abbot's residence is moss and the other half is made of white sand (p. 51). In the study hall there is a tearoom called Sakumu-ken which was greatly loved by Musashi Jouo.

Ryogen-in is the central temple of the Southern school of the Daitoku-ji sect of Zen, whose residence house was built at almost the same time as the residence house of Daisen-in. Its northern garden is called Ryogin-tei (p. 51) with the fine stones representing the Buddhist mountain of paradise, Shumisen. To the east of the hall there is a tiny garden of only about 15 square meters named Toteki-ko, and although quite small, its few rocks and white sand are quite beautiful. This might serve as an excellent model for a home garden with equally limited space.

Sangen-in was constructed by Ishida Mitsunari (1560–1600). The plain and light garden lies to the east of the abbot's residence (p. 51). The teahouse called Koan was modeled after Ennan teahouse belonging to the Yabuuchi family, which was the favorite of Yabuuchi Kennaka. It is called Koan, that is, bamboo-grove hermitage, because much bamboo was used in its construction. Furuta Oribe's grave and tombstone lie in the cemetery of this temple.

Another subtemple within the Daitoku-ji compound, Zuiho-in, was built by Otomo Sorin who was a Christian *daimyo* from Kyushu. The southern garden of the abbot's residence (p. 51) and the other gardens were all constructed by Shigemori Mirei. The southern garden called Dokuza-tei (the garden for sitting alone) is a dry landscape garden in the *Shumisen* style, and uses as a major theme or point of interest a miniature mountain called Zuiho (the auspicious mountain). The north garden is called Kanmin-tei (the garden of idle sleep). They are both fine gardens and are well taken care of.

Ashikaga Yoshimitsu's villa, Kitayama-den, which later became Rokuon-ji temple, popularly called Kinkaku-ji, that is,

Rokuon-ji (from *Miyako-Rinsen-Meisho-Zue*)

the temple of Gold Pavilion, was under construction in 1397 and by the following year the Gold Pavilion was completed. From that time many other halls and buildings were built around the Gold Pavilion and Yoshimitsu enjoyed many parties in great splendor like a crowned head of royalty. The original precious Gold Pavilion was unfortunately burned down in 1952 and it was reconstructed as the Gold Pavilion of Showa. However, the large pond garden (p. 52) surrounded by the green background of Mt. Kinugasa is beautiful as it reflects the lovely pavilion. The large island facing the Gold Pavilion is a *horai* paradise island and its pine trees are of a lovely shape and form. It was constructed together with the crane and tortoise islands with superb technique. The arrangement of *kusen-hakkai* (nine mountains and eight seas) style of the rock islands is also impressive. The rocks of Ryumon-baku waterfall, named after an actual waterfall in China, are imposing and the teahouses Kohokuro and Sekkatei (reconstructed in the Meiji era), which were dearly loved by Kanamori Sowa, are refined.

Ryumon-baku of
Kinkaku-ji

Western Kyoto

In western Kyoto one must first begin with Ryoan-ji temple. In 1450 Hosokawa Katsumoto, a governor-general of the Ashikaga government, took over a mountain villa belonging to the Tokudaiji clan and ten years later founded Daiunzan Ryoan-ji temple which was destroyed by fire during the Onin Civil War (1467-77). Katsumoto's son, Masamoto, carried out his father's plan and reconstructed the abbot's residence in 1499, at which time, it is believed, the garden (p. 53) was also constructed.

Connoisseurs of Japanese gardens have long considered Ryoan-ji garden the best of all the superb dry landscape gardens and have greatly admired its exquisite arrangement of rocks. This evaluation still holds true even in these days when garden visiting has become much more common and in vogue. Apart from the problem as to just how the garden expresses and represents Zen thought, countless numbers of people's hearts and minds have been captured by its excellence and unfathomable charm. Ordinarily a garden is called a rock garden where the focal point is the arrangement of rocks, but here at Ryoan-ji temple the rocks are distributed throughout the garden causing the focal point to be on the garden as a whole, proving emphatically its depth and the width of its charm. The effect of the total garden is to put the focal point in the heart of each visitor.

Toji-in temple has often complained of its ill-fortune from

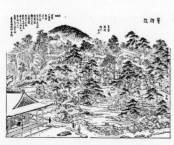

Toji-in (from *Miyako-Rinsen-Meisho-Zue*)

the end of the Edo period down to the end of World War II. After the war as life returned to normalcy, the historical evaluation of the founder of the temple, Ashikaga Takauji, greatly improved and the temple underwent considerable repair. The pond to the east, which is in the form of the Chinese character for heart, will be a quiet, elegant garden in the course of time. Seirentei teahouse, which is on the mound to the north of the pond, is matchless in the beauty of its sturdy stone steps and its *buke-doko* style of architecture (*buke* means literally *samurai* so *buke-doko* means a teahouse in the *buke* style).

Myoshin-ji temple in western Kyoto is considered to be a twin star Zen temple to Daitoku-ji temple which is located in the northern part of central Kyoto. The arrangement of halls and subtemples at Myoshin-ji is noted for its thoroughly consistent harmony.

Myoshin-ji

The west garden of Taizo-in temple (p. 55) was included in the *Miyako-Rinsen-Meisho-Zue* (Pictures of Famous Scenic Gardens of Kyoto) with an inscription that "it was constructed by master painter, Kano Motonobu, and it is a matchless garden." The picture of this garden included in the above collection is scarcely different from the present garden.

Gyokuho-in was the temple in which the Emperor Hanazono practiced Zen under the priest Muso Daishi after he had turned his villa into the temple Myoshin-ji. For that reason Gyokuho-in, which is of course in the Myoshin-ji compound, is called the holy cradle of Myoshin-ji temple. The dry landscape garden (p. 56) surrounds Gyokuho-Zengu hall and the founder's hall Misho-an.

Daishin-in temple was founded by Hosokawa Masamoto of Ryoan-ji temple. Because it had formerly been the studio of the late Sato Gengen, the sculptor, there is a peony garden here which he dearly loved (p. 57). In addition there is a lovely garden, Aun-tei, and the garden of study hall which was constructed by Mr. Nakane. The gardens are all new but they blend well into the atmosphere of the ancient temple.

The garden of Keishun-in temple (p. 57) has long been a well-known and lovely garden and it is believed to have been made by Gyokuenbo, one of the disciples of Enshu. The composition of this garden is very fine: it has a large, unique, well-trimmed tree near the veranda of the south garden of the abbot's residence and the valleylike scene beneath the tree is superb. From here, the garden winds around to the east and becomes the *roji* garden of the teahouse, Kihaku-ken.

From the beginning Japanese gardens were primarily constructed by their owners. In the late Heian period certain priests who were known as *ishitate-so* became actively engaged in the construction of gardens. However, their work was largely carried out as an avocation over and beyond their responsibilities and vocation as religious priests. In the Kamakura period the number of these gardening priests greatly increased and the number associated with Ninna-ji temple was great. Later in the Nanbokucho period the figure of Muso Kokushi appeared, though he was so great that we hesitate to label him as a gardening priest. In the Muromachi period a group of men who specialized in garden making and construction came into existence and they were known as *senzui-kawara-mono*. They were also called *niwashi* or *niwamono*. Zen'ami, who was favored by Yoshimasa, was one of them and gradually other such *senzui-kawara-mono* played active roles in the construction of gardens and Kentei and others appeared.

The garden of Ninna-ji temple (p. 58) is located to the north of the Shinden hall of the central temple. This is all that remains from the Nanbokucho period. In 1690 the garden was remodeled by Shirai Tosho and Kaku Doi and it was repaired again more recently in the second year of the Emperor Taisho (1913). The Shinden is an elegant and magnificent hall which reflects the dignity of the former Omuro Palace. The pond garden is in beautiful harmony with the hall.

Of the gardens in the Saga area, the garden of Tenryu-ji temple (p. 60) must be mentioned first. After the construction of the garden at Saiho-ji, Muso Kokushi did his utmost to make this garden, a large pond garden which lies to the west of the residence hall with a tortoise mound and a borrowed background scene of Arashiyama in the distance. There is an elegance to the beach, rock islands in the pond, and on the other side of the pond there is a unique rock formation which forms a dry waterfall, and a bridge of natural stone lying before it. Every detail is excellent and it is not an exaggeration to label it as uncomparable. The whole garden scene brings to mind a Yamato-e painting and the arrangement of rocks is said to be in the *Sogen-sansui* style (mountains and rivers as drawn in the Chinese Sung-Yuan style) of Zen temples. The garden which appears to be almost a divinely created work is a true manifestation of Muso's versatile genius. The stones of the rock waterfall especially seem to symbolize his ideal Tenka-Ryumon. It means literally the Dragon Gate of Heaven which came from the idea of the carp struggling upstream against the falling water of the waterfall with great strength and becoming a dragon; that is, the idea of attaining the heart of heaven with the waterfall as its gate. The rock islands stand

Tenryu-ji (from *Miyako-Rinsen-Meisho-Zue*)

for the solemn world of the Buddhist mountain of paradise, Shumisen.

Nison-in temple (p. 62) and Gio-ji temple (p. 63) at the foot of Mt. Ogura instill us with special emotion. They are best visited in the spring and fall when they are most beautiful but a visit when they are clothed in summer green or even on a dreary winter day can also be rewarding.

Deep in the mountains, Kozan-ji temple located in the area called Toganoö (p. 64) retains a most quiet atmosphere, which one could only find not so far from the civic center in an ancient city like Kyoto. The view from the residence hall, Sekisui-in, presents a superb view of nature surpassing that of the excellent but man-made garden. The plain building of Sekisui-in hall, which is an official National Treasure, harmonizes well both with the nearby garden scene and with the scenery in the distance. There is no word appropriate enough to describe the total picture except that it is wonderful.

View from Sekisui-in

From Toganoö as one walks toward Shuzan along the road which leads into the deep mountains, one comes to the mountain country temple of Joshoko-ji (p. 65). In early April when cherry blossoms are in bloom many come to admire in silence the graceful tree which is called Kokonoe-zakura and another famous cherry tree called Kuruma-gaeshi-no-sakura. The appearance of the halls and the grounds of this temple which was founded by the retired emperor Kogon deep within the mountains impress us with an even deeper sense of respect for him. There are also lovely old pine trees and camellia trees which are planted around his mountain tomb, a setting which he preferred to the regular kind of setting and tomb which he could have had as a former emperor.

To the south of Moss Temple (nickname for Saiho-ji) at Kinugasa-san, one finds the temple Jizo-in, whose garden (p. 67) is believed to have been the one especially loved by Hosokawa Yoriyuki, a teacher and adviser to Yoshimitsu. The rocks which are carefully placed around the garden on the moss-covered ground are believed to represent the sixteen disciples of Buddha on a pilgrimage. One can feel familiarity and closeness toward this plain and unaffected garden.

Southern Kyoto

The shrine, Jonangu at Fushimi-Toba, and Gokogu-jinja shrine at Momoyama both have lovely gardens made by Nakane Kinsaku. The retired emperor Shirakawa's Toba Imperial Villa, or Toba-den, occupied a large area which extended to the area now known as Takeda. At its center was the present shrine Jonangu (p. 70). In this wide area there once stood many halls with a wonderful pond garden. Recently a report of the excavation of the ruins of Toba-den was announced.

The western garden adjoining the study and office of Gokogu shrine (p. 71) is a dry landscape rock garden related to Kobori Enshu, who became the Magistrate of Fushimi in 1623 at the age of 45 and held the position for some twenty years. He made the gardens on his own will and initiative within the grounds around the Magistrate's office and then invited the shogun Tokugawa Iemitsu to stay here when he visited Kyoto in 1634. After the Second World War the garden was destroyed completely, but the priest of the shrine fortunately did not dispose of the precious rocks of the older garden but instead used them as the basis for his construction of the present garden. The garden reflects the talent and genius of Kobori Enshu who left a history of accomplishments and weakness at Fushimi and it will no doubt be discussed long into the future.

The pond garden of Byodo-in temple (p. 74) was at one time a very large garden which was frequently visited by emperors who enjoyed themselves here with music and song. In the course of time, however, the pond was made smaller and smaller, and on the ground that was formerly part of the pond Saisho-in and Jodo-in were built. According to the *Miyako-Meisho-Zue* (Pictures of Famous Places in Kyoto) which was published in 1780, the garden was previously much larger than it is today and it presented a fine view. In the caption for the colored picture which appears in this book I refer to the garden for observation from the hall rather than for strolling because the present garden is of that type.

Shuon-an temple is worth remembering as a holy place associated with the Zen priest and chief priest of the temple, Ikku (1394–1481). It was here that he died at the age of eighty-eight and was buried. The garden (p. 75) represents the pilgrimage of the 16 disciples of Buddha but the large solid rock is the main focal point of the garden. Other stones and rocks are also heavy and magnificent and they have been carefully placed according to the Shumisen or *horai* style of rock grouping. Behind the stones the view of a distant field has been borrowed, but most recently its effect on the mood and beauty of the garden has been reduced.

Gardens of Other Districts in Japan

Enman-in is a high-ranking temple which holds many famous and historical articles in addition to having a lovely garden.

Byodo-in (from *Miyako-Meisho-Zue*)

This garden is a pond garden with a miniature hill, a typical representative garden of the early Edo period. The tortoise island shown in the picture (p. 78) seems to have been added in later years. The bridge in the garden has been damaged some but the garden itself is excellent, demonstrating the superb technique of its builder. The view of an old cherry tree on the miniature hill as seen from the Shinden hall reminds one of the atmosphere which prevailed at courtly parties of princes and *daimyo*.

The well called Hashiri-i of Gesshin-ji temple was located under the eaves of a tearoom and was greatly favored by travelers. The pond garden (p. 79) was constructed in the mid-Edo period but was later remodeled by the painter Hashimoto Kansetsu.

Shoju Raigo-ji is an old temple related to Mt. Hiei. It is also related to Akechi Mitsuhide (1528–82). The garden (p. 80) was built by Soshin who was Mitsuhide's retainer. Soshin was a master of the art of flower arrangement, and the dry landscape garden here which he constructed is unique. The garden beneath the low stone bridge is covered with moss and represents, it is believed, a "dry" pond. However, apart from the unique style of flower arrangement, this seemingly "dry" garden is provided with stepping stones—a technique quite unusual in the ordinary dry garden.

The residential temples of Sakamoto have almost always had gardens with running streams. The garden of Ritsu-in temple (p. 81) was made in the early Edo period. Even so it is cared for so well that it looks as fresh and neat as if it had only been completed a few days ago. These gardens in the temples of this area are believed to have been built by the priests who lived in the temples at the time the gardens were constructed.

The garden of the former Shurin-ji (p. 81), the present Kosho-ji temple, was made, as they believe at the temple, by Hosokawa Takakuni in order to comfort Ashikaga Yoshiharu who had escaped from the wars which had been raging at the time and lived under the protection of the Kuchiki clan.

The trimmed-bush garden of Daichi-ji temple (p. 82) has come to be well known as a garden constructed by Kobori Enshu, while the garden of Fukuju-ji temple (p. 83) has not yet come to be very well known among garden lovers. The latter temple was constructed in the early Heian period on Mt. Ganzo and the garden which was made after the revival of the temple uses only the natural stones found on this mountain above. Each time a step is climbed the view of the garden varies. It is more than likely that the stones represent images of Buddha. When one finally reaches the top of the mountain one realizes even more deeply the outstanding artistic merit of this garden.

At the garden of Matsuo-jinja shrine (p. 83) the magnificent rock arrangements which represent *horai* paradise stretch from the ground in front of the shrine office to the foot of a mountain. They are a fine, pioneering example of the Momoyama period.

The gardens of the temples on the eastern side of Lake Biwa have their own distinct character: there is a deep quietude about the garden of Kongorin-ji (p. 84) and a unique elaboration about the garden of Saimyo-ji (p. 85). The former has stones and trees at a higher level from the pond and the latter has a dry waterfall on the opposite side of the pond with carefully placed rocks deep to the back of a miniature hill.

In Hikone City are two fine gardens, one, a pond garden called Genkyu-en (p. 86) which belongs to the city and the other, a dry landscape garden called Rakuraku-en (p. 87) which belongs to a restaurant of the same name. The latter is not open to the public but is for the pleasure of customers to the restaurant.

Ryotan-ji temple is located to the north of Hikone City. The temple has a long association with garden construction and once offered very rare instruction in the art of garden making. Probably this was related to the training of Buddhist priests who possessed special skill in garden construction. The first priest of the temple, the Zen priest Koten, was the founder and senior teacher. As a result, the south garden of the abbot's residence (p. 88) and the east garden of the study hall (p. 89) were quite unique. In fact the south garden is probably the finest of all the dry landscape gardens of the early Edo period.

The stepping stones in the pond (*sawatari*) in the east garden of the study hall are splendid but also noteworthy is the set of multiple rocks which makes up the dry waterfall. At the top of a hill, there are monuments erected for the repose of the souls of Muso Kokushi, Kobori Enshu, and the Zen priest Koten, all great garden makers, since Zen discipline was practiced here through garden making.

The temple Seigan-ji belongs to the Soto sect of Zen Buddhism. The garden of Seigan-ji (p. 89), which includes a dry pond, is surrounded by the priest's quarters, the abbot's residence and the study hall. The miniature hill in the center of the dry pond is the *horai* island. The rocks of the dry waterfall and other rocks throughout the garden are arranged beautifully and the scene of trimmed bushes and trees is wonderful.

Ground of Kongorin-ji

The dry pond is covered by heavy moss and the trimmed bush beneath the bridge of hewn stone is quite effective.

Jiko-in temple is located on the top of a hill outside of Koriyama, Nara. Its garden is so lovely that visitors are often so attracted by the large trimmed-bush garden and the view beyond that they forget to notice the central hall in which they stand (p. 92). The stone-paved approach called Arare-Ishijiki leads to the plain and placid study hall. The unique design of this garden, including the choice of the land with its natural scenic beauty, the formation of the miniature hill by means of the trimmed bushes, and the architecture of the study hall, is far beyond the ability of common man and causes one but to wonder at its magnificence.

Isui-en garden which is located in Nara has a pond and the interesting stepping stones in the pond are mill stones (p. 92–93). The background view is beautiful.

The garden of Shido-dera temple in Shikoku (p. 95), which had flowing water as a *kyokusui*-style garden and was closely related to its creator Hosokawa Yoriyuki, was completely devastated but was repaired and remodeled by Mr. Shigemori in 1953.

Eiho-ji temple of Tajimi City in Chubu District was once Muso Kokushi's villa. The garden pond (p. 104) in front of the Goddess of Mercy Pavilion with the bridge called Musaikyo which spans the pond is all that remains of the original villa. Together they bring to mind the past when Muso first built the garden.

At Erin-ji temple in Yamanashi Prefecture the garden is built around a pond in the shape of the Chinese character for heart. The rocks on a small garden mound are wonderfully arranged and the garden scenes (p. 106), including a small waterfall, are lush and rich.

SUGGESTIONS FOR MAKING A JAPANESE GARDEN

The Heart and Will Make a Garden

In lectures which I gave on garden tours I used to say to the visitors: "What you should try to do is to adopt the interesting feature of the garden into your own garden. Anyone can begin by making gradual changes in their existing gardens, and then going on to make the whole design of the garden. At first feel free to imitate what is good and excellent in other gardens, and then after initial changes are made in your own garden, you will more than likely be dissatisfied with mere imitation and you will have begun to learn by degrees the technique of constructing a garden incorporating your own ideas. The garden then becomes your own. This is true even if you have begun by fascination with and imitation of a famous garden. Your final result is an original garden with an independent entity. If not, the garden remains simply an imitation and cannot be said to be yours."

In addition I also often spoke to the visitors about a small garden called Totekiko to the east of the abbot's residence of Ryogen-in temple within the compound of Daitoku-ji. The garden space is quite small, surrounded by the temple buildings. Such a garden in such a small space is called *tsubo* or *tsubo niwa*. The space here is less than ten square meters but nevertheless there is a garden of raked white sand and five stones arranged in two groups. Named Totekiko (Eastern Water-drop Jar), the garden symbolizes that the stronger the power by which a stone is thrown in the water, the larger will the ripples be. This is suggested by the rings or waves, which are created by a single drop which falls into the sea. Apart from understanding this or knowing its symbolism, the raked sand is not at all monotonous and the total work of art created by the white sand and the fine rocks has something which appeals to one's heart. Such a small space which can be found almost anywhere can thus be turned into a lovely garden. I wish to emphasize that to make a good garden does not depend on the width of the space. A space as small as two meters square can be made into a fine garden in accordance and harmony with its surroundings. In other words in even the smallest space, if with your heart and will you desire to build a garden, it is possible to make a fine garden suitable to that site.

Totekiko of Ryogen-in

How to Adopt Traditional Beauty

The first important consideration of making a garden is the space available. One must carefully take into account how the garden will look after completion, considering the shape and width of the garden to be built. Then considering how the garden will harmonize with the house, the adjoining buildings, and with other surroundings, the ground should be selected and a plan and possibly a blueprint should be drawn up. Since you are more than likely not a specialist, it is probable that on your first attempt you may wish to set to work at once without the time involved in making a blueprint for construction. Let us nevertheless, here, narrow our field of concentration to a consideration of making a garden for one's home.

Four kinds of gardens must be mentioned here, which have become common in the tradition of the Japanese garden since the mid-Edo period: first, a garden with water in a pond or stream; second, a dry landscape garden in which no water is used; third, a teahouse garden, and finally, a *sukiya* garden which is a variation of the teahouse garden.

Suppose one wishes to make a garden with a pond. A small waterfall and a stream may also be desired. To make the waterfall one must arrange the rocks at different levels to give the feeling of actual flowing water. According to the *Sakuteiki* (Manual of Garden Making), one of the oldest manuals of garden making, there are various very old methods of arranging the rocks, such as by making steps somewhere between the top and the base or by making the rocks look like fallen cloth, that is, a *nuno-ochi* style of stone arrangement. You may want to make an island in the pond and connect it to the shore with a bridge. Of course one must calculate the layout as a whole and the expense involved in the construction and the materials. What is required is a careful thinking through of the means by which you will express the feeling you wish to convey and the way this will best be accomplished. As an example let us direct our attention to the group of rocks in the waterfall which is called Shiraito-no-taki, located in a corner of the garden of Jugetsukan in the lower garden at Shugakuin Imperial Villa. From this waterfall a stream flows across the garden. Small as it is in scope, it is refined and elegant, and well worthy of study.

Shiraito-no-taki at
Shugakuin Rikyu

Another small, simple waterfall is found in the eastern corner of the garden at Shisen-do villa. The water from it runs quietly beneath the trimmed bushes and beside the outer porch with graceful elegance. There is no pond attached to this stream and it is thus not so difficult to make such a stream. Another example is the small pond garden east of the study hall at Rinkyu-ji temple. The stones of the waterfall are arranged at the foot of a hill surrounded by trimmed azalea bushes. These examples suggest that a garden with a pond or waterfall can be constructed beautifully and elegantly without making a large-scale garden. One may create a waterfall scene with the use of a single rock with water flowing over it, or one may flow water into the garden through a picturesque bamboo pipe.

A dry landscape (*kare-sansui*) garden does not require water at all. The most typical example is the garden of Daisen-in temple which is the best of this type although its width is only 100 square meters.

A *kare-sansui* garden is convenient and economical for us to make, for it can be constructed in a very small space without the use of water. As many are aware, a number of *kare-sansui* gardens were the product of a novel technique which exhibited to the full extent the traditional manner of Japanese gardens. Typically *kare-sansui* characteristics and its plain beauty are also revealed in the garden of the study room of Reiun-in and the *tsubo-niwa* of Tokai-an, both within the compound of Myoshin-ji temple. One can learn much from these gardens.

Teahouse gardens, which were first built in the Momoyama period, have frequently been constructed since its beginning because the feeling of simplicity and the simple elegance and technique of the gardens have captured the feelings and attention of countless people. The teahouse garden which is particularly appropriate for teahouses built in the hut style, represents and brings to mind, according to Rikyu, the approach to a mountain temple.

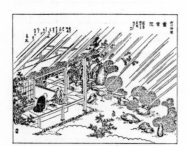

Reiun-in (from *Miyako-Rinsen-Meisho-zue*)

Trees

One of the most essential elements of a garden which comes to anyone's mind is the tree. However, many *kare-sansui* gardens have no trees and not a single blade of grass, as the garden of Ryoan-ji temple and others illustrate. In a Japanese garden emphasis is placed on the importance of rocks, and these rocks and stones are very often considered to be the structural center of the garden while the trees are often regarded as fringe ornamentation.

It is often said that a garden grows. This mostly refers to the growth of the trees in a garden. If trees are added along with the important rocks, the growth of the trees often destroys the intention of the original garden design or plan. Therefore, trees of only limited growth have often been used and various methods to suppress their growth have often been employed. A further device normally adopted is to keep the bushes and trees trimmed.

Trimming is artificial. One has to choose the proper trees and bushes which can be used for this purpose. There is not only a difference in size but a difference in form according to the shape desired.

Trimmed hedge of Nishi-hama at Shugakuin Rikyo

Rock Arrangements

Besides being the structural center, rocks are also often the central focus of interest as they appear in various places and in various forms and arrangements. They are placed on a miniature hill; they are used as rock islands or as the only island of a pond; they are set on the beach; they form waterfalls and bridges. They are also used as stepping stones and, placed together they form a paved walk.

In arranging rocks as *iwagumi* rocks are generally placed in three ways: standing vertically, lying horizontally on top of the ground, and half buried in the ground. The number of rocks which are used also varies. In some cases only a single rock is used while in other cases several. In some gardens, sets of rocks and scattered rocks are used. There are thus numerous kinds of arrangements and numerous possibilities for new, original creations. However, herein lies the difficulty. One must see and study the ancient art, technique, and style of the excellent gardens. Learning from them, one can then add one's own creative thought and style. A single rock isolated from others produces an artistic effect if placed appropriately. In such a case the beauty of the single rock itself must be considered carefully.

Sand, Moss, and Lawn

Sand, moss, and grass are also important components in a Japanese garden. If the sand is found in a dry landscape garden, it usually symbolizes the sea, or a mountain stream, or a river or sometimes it merely implies a dry pond or brook. Though sand was also used in the pond gardens of the Heian period, the symbolic use of sand that characterizes the dry landscape gardens which have been made since the Muromachi period, marked the real beginning of a new technique with new material in Japanese gardens. Sometimes even colored sand has been used to create a special desired effect. Usually various designs and patterns are made in the sand with a special rake designed for the purpose. Sometimes the sand is built up into a mound so that the designs and patterns are made on the flat top, the most typical examples being that which are found at the temple of Silver Pavilion.

Sand is also used in small gardens and those known as *tsubo-niwa*. Whereas moss and grass require a great deal of attention sand is relatively easy to care for. Sometimes in these small gardens gravel or small pebbles are used instead of sand. For teahouse gardens moss has an almost indispensable place. No other material or substance seems to be as suitable to cover the bare ground and give a soothing effect to the garden. A view of stepping stones buried deep in moss which lies as a covering over the ground is very charming. It seems safe to

Checker pattern made on the sand at Tofuku-ji

Mounds of sand at Honen-in

Patterns made by moss at Sanbo-in

Hewn stone bridge in Kokei-no-Niwa at Nishi Hongan-ji

Earthen bridge at Sanbo-in

Stepping stones at Konchi-in

say that the *wabi* (simple, quiet taste) feeling one senses in a Japanese garden is largely due to the presence of moss.

In addition to growing in its natural surroundings, moss can be transplanted and nurtured in other places where one desires. However, it is important that they are weeded and watered every morning and evening. A large amount of water is needed, especially in the summer when there is little rain.

Although lawn has been used in Japanese gardens from time past, there is something about it which brings to mind Western gardens. The gardens which adjoined the large *daimyo* mansions usually had lawn around the ponds and on the small mounds or hills.

Water

The three main components of a garden are rocks, trees, and water. Water is not only an indispensable part of nature in its natural setting but also extremely important for gardens. Whatever newer type gardens were developed, the idea still remains that ponds have a central place in gardens. Sometimes waterfalls and brooks have been actually made and at other times as we find in the dry landscape gardens, at least since the Muromachi period, water has been symbolically represented by rocks and sand. Though quite different in technique, both the pond garden and the dry landscape garden reveal our yearning for the sea.

Bridges

The material by which bridges are made are rocks and wood and sometimes there are even bridges which are covered by the earth. Irrespective of whether or not there is actually water over which they cross, they span ponds, brooks or streams flowing from waterfalls. Garden bridges are used primarily for aesthetic purposes rather than for their practical use, although public gardens often have bridges which suit both purposes. The material and form should be decided according to how the bridge will be used, or what function the bridge will have.

Stepping Stones and Paved Stones

One of the principal components of teahouse gardens are the set of stepping stones or paved stones which make up the path. They were first used in order that one's *geta* (wooden clogs) or *zori* (slippers) would not get wet while walking along the teahouse garden. Their primary purpose can then be said to be practical, and only secondarily aesthetic. Gradually, however,

Stepping stones at Katsura Rikyu

more and more emphasis has been placed on their aesthetic quality. As with the other components of a garden there are various ways of setting the stepping stones, that is, two to a group, three or four to a group, and even those which are set in the form or shape of flying wild geese or flying plovers. Most stones are placed in the garden in their natural form but sometimes hewn stones are also used.

Often instead of having a bridge, stepping stones are used to cross a pond or brook. These stones are called *sawatari-ishi*, that is, water-crossing stones, or *sawatobi-ishi*, that is, water-jumping stones. Examples of such water-crossing stones are those which are found in the pond garden at Heian Shrine (p. 19) and in that at Hakusa-sonso (p. 25) and in that at Isui-en (p. 92-93) in Nara. Stones which are used to cross brooks are found everywhere.

The paved stone path, which is called in Japanese *nobedan*, is used in the approach to the garden or on the path around the garden for convenience in walking. It therefore serves both a practical and aesthetic purpose.

There are also different styles for the arrangement of paved stones according to the principles derived from the tea ceremony, that is, the *shin, gyo,* and *so* styles. *So* refers to the style which uses natural stones; the combination of natural stones with hewn stones is called *gyo,* and *shin* refers to the style which uses only hewn stones. Stepping stones and paved stones are found in almost every garden. One should study them and apply the ideas and feeling gained as one plans and builds one's own garden.

Fences and Hedges

Fences and hedges are likewise differentiated according to their purpose. As one would imagine they too serve both for practical and aesthetic reasons. Ordinarily garden fences and hedges are in two categories of classifications as their name implies, simply hedges and fences made of bamboo. There are likewise two categories of bamboo fences, *kakoi-gaki* fence, or a fence which surrounds the garden, and *sode-gaki* fence. The former includes *Ken'nin-ji-gaki, Katsura-gaki* (see the picture on the left), *Koetsu-gaki* (p. 37), and *Ginkaku-ji-gaki. Ken'nin-ji-gaki* sets the basic design for bamboo fences and its variant style is named after the temple in which it is found. Sometimes one finds in addition to the above type fences, those which are made from spicebush, bush clover, or scouring rush. Such a fence is called *shiba-gaki,* or grass fence. The *sode-gaki* fence is used to define the boundary of the ground and has the func-

Ginkaku-ji-gaki

Katsura-gaki at Katsura Rikyu

Sode-gaki fence of
Shisen-do

Oribe style lantern
at Katsura Rikyu

Sanko-toro at Katsura Rikyu

Renge-ji style lantern

tion of shutting out any external distracting view, thus enhancing and emphasizing the elegant effect of the garden. There are also a number of styles of this type fence as well. Materials of fences which are used for modern houses need to be more durable. Even so, these materials must also be in harmony with the house and the garden if they are to serve an aesthetic as well as a practical function.

Lanterns and Stone Water Basins

The lanterns are made of stone, metal, or other materials. The major styles of the garden lanterns for old temple and shrine use are the *Kasuga,* the *Byodo-in,* the *Hannya-ji,* the *Koto-in* and the *Renge-ji* types. Teahouse garden lanterns are of the triangle, the *yukimi* (lantern to appreciate snow in the garden), the *Oribe* and the *sode* (the lantern in the shape of a kimono sleeve) types. There are an especially great many variations of lanterns loved by the masters of the tea ceremony.

There is no particular rule for placing lanterns in the garden, but needless to say, it is important to have it placed in a position harmonious to the rest of the garden. Usually a smaller lantern is used for a small garden and conversely a larger one is used in a large garden. Sometimes, however, a particular effect can be created by using a small lantern in a large garden and a large one in a small garden. The use of too many lanterns, however, is not advisable but shows rather poor taste. The original purpose of the stone lantern was to lighten the area around the water basin in the garden or it was placed to lighten and indicate the location of the garden path. Lanterns are most often used together with trees or bushes and are either displayed half-hidden or in full view according to the purpose or intention desired.

In the gardens of private homes a stone lantern may be used to unify the whole garden by making it the focus of interest, or a small garden may be constructed with the use of a lantern and very little else. In such a garden the use of trees is not advisable but instead one might use lawn or moss as well as a few carefully trimmed bushes. It can be safely assumed that a good rule to follow in using a lantern is to consider first of all its primary function, that is, to give light. With this in mind the first step in its proper and appropriate placement is made.

Water basins, although sometimes made from other materials, are most often made out of stone. They are classified into two categories according to the place where they are to be used, the *chozubachi* basin and the *tsukubai* basin. The *chozubachi* basin is always placed close to the outer porch and contains

Water basin at Raigo-ji

water which is used for washing hands. For this reason it is rather high. In some cases *chozubachi* basins are placed only as ornaments and serve no other function beyond their aesthetic one. *Tsukubai* basins, on the other hand, are an indispensable part of the teahouse garden for the very reason that they enhance the charm of the garden. They may, however, be set at any place in the garden where they can best fulfill that function.

The simple combination of a water basin with either a stone lantern or a tree can produce a quite refined atmosphere and an excellent scene, surpassing even some of the more elaborately constructed gardens.

An essential factor in the making of garden is to have a deep love toward the materials and components and to place them in such a way that they will have a unified and harmonious effect in the total scheme of the garden. Similar to other fields of art, the final beauty of a garden is attributable to the humanity or artistic creativity of the creator.

Glossary of Garden Terms

Here are some Japanese garden terms including those which deal with minor but important items and those which have not been explained in the text. Some terms which are only indirectly related to the garden have also been included.

agesudo : A kind of wicket in the teahouse garden. This wicket, also called *hajitomi*, is used as a gate which divides the teahouse garden into the inner and outer sections.

bukeshoin-zukuri : An architectural style used in the mansions of the *samurai (buke)* class.

chozubachi : A water basin containing water for handwashing before the tea ceremony. A stone water basin serves as an effective accessory of the garden.

chumon : A simple gate or wicket in the garden.

dejima : Peninsula made in the garden pond.

enzanseki : A rock or rocks which serves to represent a distant scene of mountains. They are placed on the upper part of the miniature hill or mound.

fumi-ishi : The stepping stone which lies closest to the entrance of the teahouse. Since the first step is made on this stone when leaving the teahouse, it is also called the *ichiban-ishi* (the first stone). The second stone is called the *ochi-ishi* and the third stone is the *nori-ishi*.

fumiwake-ishi : A stone which is set where the line of stepping stones is forked. A stone larger than the others, especially a *garan-seki* (see below) is often used.

funa-ishi : Also called *funagata-ishi*. This is a stone in the form of a ship in gardens built in the *horai* style (see below), whether that of a pond garden or that of a dry landscape garden. The *funa-ishi* is placed differently according to whether it stands for an outgoing ship on its way to *horai* paradise island or an incoming ship on its way back from *horai* island.

fusuma : A sliding door with wooden frame plastered with paper or cloth, on which, in most cases, pictures are painted.

ganto : A rock island constructed entirely of a single rock or set of rocks in a garden pond.

garan-seki : Foundation stone of a temple. In a garden it is often used as a corner stone in a group of stepping stones where a larger stone is needed. It is sometimes made into a water basin with a bowl-like indentation made in the top to contain water.

gogan : Rocks which border a pond.

hachimae : A set of rocks around the water basin through which the water drains.

haiku : A poem of 17 syllables.

hira-niwa : A flat garden with no pond and no mound.

horai-jima : An island in the middle of a garden pond which represents the sea. The island, *horai-jima*, symbolizes the ideal world of perennial youth and immortality.

ido : This simply means a well, but in relationship to a garden an *ido* refers to a well made within the garden. It serves primarily as an ornament or as a point of interest in the garden, for the edges of its wall are usually made in an interesting form. Sometimes lanterns, bushes, trees, or rocks are placed next to it or nearby and the top is often covered with a lid of bamboo stalks fastened together with string.

iwakura: A rock or a group of rocks serving as the object of worship.

iwasaka: The ground where the rocks of *iwakura* (see above) are set.

kaiyu-shiki garden: A type of pond garden in which paths are made around the pond and through the whole garden for the enjoyment of strolling.

kakehi (or, more commonly called simply *kakei*): A device whereby water is led through a pipe of bamboo stalks to a water basin. A *kakehi* is usually elegant and tasteful and produces the pleasant or rhythmical sound of flowing water.

kansho-shiki garden: A type which is represented in both pond and dry landscape gardens. The chief point of interest for *kansho-shiki* gardens is the view obtained from the study room or some other building. The paths in the garden, if provided, are not for practical use.

kare-ike: Dry pond, that is, a pond which does not have or require water. It is used in a dry landscape style of garden.

kare-nagare: A dry stream, that is, a stream which does not use water. The river or stream bed is covered either with sand, gravel, or moss. Some are equipped with stepping stones and a bridge.

kare-sansui garden: A dry landscape garden, in which water is not used.

karikomi: Either a trimmed tree or bush.

kesa style: A style of stone lantern.

koshikake-machiai: A small shelter where guests wait for the host within the teahouse garden before the tea ceremony which is about to be held in the teahouse or tearoom. If the shelter lies within the inner garden it is called an *uchi* (inner) *koshikake,* and if it is outside of the inner garden it is called *soto* (outside) *koshikake.*

kusen-hakkai: The nine mountains and eight seas around Mt. Shumisen (see below), the highest ideal mountain of Buddhism. In the garden they are represented by a garden pond and an island of either a single stone or a group of stones.

kutsunugi-ishi: A large flat stone placed beneath the step of the study hall or guest hall or the teahouse upon which to leave one's *geta* (wooden clogs) or shoes. This is found even in the gardens of private houses.

kyaku-seki (or, *kyaku-ishi*): A stone which is set just outside of the middle gate of the teahouse garden. An example is found in the picture on page 44. In a tea ceremony the chief guest (*kyaku*) greets the host while standing or crouching on this stone. Hence the name *kyaku-ishi.*

kyokusui-shiki garden: This refers to a style of garden with a winding riverlike stream running through the garden. This style which was imported from China was applied to the Japanese gardens of the Heian period and the parties which were held on boats floating in the *kyokusui* gardens were considered by the nobles to be the most elegant. On the boats the nobles would sip wine and write poems.

mizuwake-ishi: A rock placed toward the foot of a waterfall on which the falling water is separated, hence the name *mizuwake-ishi* (literally, water-separating rock).

nakakuguri: A simple gate which divides the *roji* (see below) into the inner and the outer section.

nagare-tsukubai: This is a water basin placed within a running stream or on the bank.

niwa-mon: Garden gate. Made for its artistic effect as well as for its practical purpose.

nobedan: A stone-paved path in the garden.

nunoochi: A technique of arranging the rocks of a waterfall so that the falling stream of water may remain undivided.

roji: A garden leading to and around the teahouse.

Ryumon-baku: The name of a waterfall in the upper Huang Ho River (Yellow River) in China. This waterfall is represented in dry landscape gardens by a set of rocks which is called Ryumon-no-taki.

sanson-iwagumi: A set of three rocks which represent three Buddhist images. The *sanson* rocks are classified according to what they represent: *Shaka-sanzon* (including Shaka [Buddha] followed by two saints), *Yakushi-sanzon* (Yakushi, the Central Buddhist God of the Eastern Paradise, followed by Nikko and Gekko Buddhist gods), and *Amida-sanzon* (Amida, the Central Buddhist God of the Western Paradise, followed by Kannon and Seishi Buddhist gods). The central stone of the three is larger than the others.

sekido: A kind of stone work built in the shape of a hexagonal or octagonal column. It resembles a stone lantern but at the place where a light would burn in a lantern, there is instead an engraved Buddhist image. It is an object of prayer.

sen'yu-shiki garden: A type of pond garden such as the large pond gardens which were built in the Heian period for boating and boating parties.

shakkei: A term to describe the borrowing of a distant scene outside of the garden for the garden's background. Such a combination of a borrowed scene with a garden scene enhances the artistic effect.

shiho-butsu: Four Buddhist images engraved on the four sides of a tombstone. Usually the images of the Buddha (called Shaka), Miroku, Yakushi, Amida, as well as others are used.

shinden-zukuri: An architectural style formerly used in the mansions of the court nobles. *Shinden* is the central hall.

shinsen: A mythological immortal being living in the mountains and well versed in mysterious arts.

shukukei: The construction in a garden of a scene of some well-known scenic spot on a smaller scale.

Shumisen: The central mountain in the ideal Buddhistic world of the nine mountains and eight seas. In the garden, Mt. Shumisen is represented by a rock standing high among a group of rocks.

sukiya-zukuri: An architectural style of teahouse which aims at producing the atmosphere of *wabi* (simple quiet taste).

sute-ishi: A rock which is placed separately from other arranged rocks. This is often found in ordinary private gardens to enhance the beauty of the garden.

tokonoma: An alcove in a Japanese room; in it a calligraphic or pictorial scroll is hung, and a vase of flowers and some ornamental object are placed.

tome-ishi: A stone placed on the garden path or on stepping stones to indicate that the path is closed. The stone is tied with a rope to identify it as such. It is also called *sekimori-ishi*.

tsuboniwa: A small garden surrounded by buildings on all sides.

tsukubai: A stone water basin which is placed in the middle of a garden. It actually consists of a set of stones, a large rock with a hollowed-out basin in the top center to hold water (water-basin stone), a rock called *mae-ishi* which is placed in front of the water-basin stone, another stone which is called *yuoke-ishi* is placed to the right of the water-basin stone and another which is called the *teshoku-ishi* on the left. Sometimes, however, formality of having each of these is disregarded.

uchi-roji: *Uchi-roji* refers to the teahouse garden inside of the middle gate, or *nakakuguri*, or middle wicket. Usually an elaborate design is devised through the teahouse garden or the approach to the teahouse.

waka: A poem of 31 syllables.

yari-mizu: Originally in the gardens of the Heian period this referred to a stream of running water flowing in a zigzag path beneath the hall called a *suiwata-dono* into the pond. Strictly speaking, *yari-mizu* was not constructed after the Kamakura period but a similar type of stream was made in later periods and is found in many gardens.

yodomari-iwagumi: A group of stones placed in a line and lying within a pond which represent ships heading toward *horai-jima,* anchored in moorage at night.

yoritsuki: One of the houses built in the outer teahouse garden in which the guests first gather together. Coming together in Japanese is expressed by the word *yoru*. Hence the name *yoritsuki*.

zazen: A discipline of Zen Buddhism in which one practices meditation, while sitting quietly in an erect posture.

Alphabetical List of Gardens

The numbers on the right refer to page numbers of plates. Macrons are given on garden names at left only.

Garden				Address	Page
Byōdō-in	平	等	院	Renge-cho, Uji City, Kyoto Pref.	*74*
Chido Museum	致 道 博 物	館	Kachushin-machi, Tsuruoka City, Yamagata Pref.	*111*
Chishaku-in	智	積	院	Higashiyama Shichijo, Kyoto	*14*
Daichi-ji	大	池	寺	Nasaka, Minakuchi-cho, Shiga Pref.	*82*
Daisen-in	大	仙	院	Daitoku-ji compound (*see* Daitoku-ji)	*48*
Daishin-in	大	心	院	Myoshin-ji compound, Hanazono, Kyoto	*57*
Daitoku-ji	大	徳	寺	Daitokuji-cho, Murasakino, Kyoto	*46*
Daitsū-ji	大	通	寺	Midomae-cho, Nagahama City, Shiga Pref.	*91*
Eihō-ji	永	保	寺	Kokei-zan, Tajimi City, Gifu Pref.	*104*
Enman-in	円	満	院	Onjoji-cho, Otsu City, Shiga Pref.	*78*
Entsū-ji	円	通	寺	Hataeda-cho, Iwakura, Kyoto	*34*
Erin-ji	恵	林	寺	Koyashiki, Shioyama City, Yamanashi Pref.	*106*
Fukada house	深 田 氏	邸	Kuzumo, Yonago City, Tottori Pref.	*99*
Fukuju-ji	福	寿	寺	Mabuchi-Iwakura, Omi-Hachiman City, Shiga Pref.	*83*
Funda-in	芬	陀	院	Tofuku-ji compound (*see* Tofuku-ji)	*12*
Genkyū-en	玄	宮	園	Konki-machi, Hikone City, Shiga Pref.	*86, 87*
Gesshin-ji	月	心	寺	Hashirii, Otani-cho, Otsu City, Shiga Pref.	*79*
Giō-ji	祇	王	寺	Ojoin-cho, Nison'in-monzen, Saga, Kyoto	*63*
Ginkaku-ji	銀	閣	寺	Ginkakuji-cho, Kyoto	*24*
Gokōgū Jinja	御 香 宮 神	社	Fushimi Momoyama-cho, Kyoto	*71*
Gyokuhō-in	玉	鳳	院	Myoshin-ji compound (*see* Daishin-in)	*56*
Hakusa-sonsō	白 沙 村	荘	Ishibashi-cho, Jodoji, Kyoto	*25*
Heian Jingū	平 安 神	宮	Nishi-Tenno-cho, Okazaki, Kyoto	*18, 19*
Higashi Hongan-ji	東 本 願	寺	Karasuma Shichijo-agaru, Kyoto	*40*
Hokke-ji	法	華	寺	Hokkeji-cho, Nara	*93*
Hōnen-in	法	然	院	Minamida-cho, Jodoji, Kyoto	*23*
Honma Art Museum	本 間 美 術	館	Onari-cho, Sakata City, Yamagata Pref.	*110*
Hōshun-in	芳	春	院	Daitoku-ji compound (*see* Daitoku-ji)	*49*

Garden					Address	Page
Hyōzu Taisha	兵	主	大	社	Gojo, Chuzu-cho, Yasu-gun, Shiga Pref.	82
Ikō-ji	醫		光	寺	Masuda-cho, Masuda City, Shimane Pref.	100
Isui-en	依		水	園	Suimon-cho, Nara	93
Jakkō-in	寂		光	院	Kusao-cho, Ohara, Kyoto	32
Jikō-in	慈		光	院	Koizumi, Yamato-Koriyama City, Nara Pref.	92
Jissō-in	実		相	院	Agura-cho, Iwakura, Kyoto	36
Jizō-in	地		蔵	院	Kitano-machi, Yamada, Kyoto	67
Jōei-ji	常		栄	寺	Miyano, Yamaguchi	103
Jōnan-gū	城		南	宮	Miyanoato-cho, Shimotoba, Kyoto	70
Jōruri-ji	浄	瑠	璃	寺	Nishiko, Kamo-cho, Kyoto Pref.	76
Jōshōkō-ji	常	照	光	寺	Ido, Yamaguni-mura, Kyoto Pref.	65
Kanshū-ji	勧		修	寺	Niodo-cho, Kanshuji, Yamashina, Kyoto	72
Katsura Rikyū	桂		離	宮	Misono-cho, Katsura, Kyoto	68, 69
Keishun-in	桂		春	院	Myoshin-ji compound (see Daishin-in)	57
Kenroku-en	兼		六	園	Dewa-cho, Kanazawa City, Ishikawa Pref.	107
Kinkaku-ji	金		閣	寺	Kinkakuji-cho Kinugasa, Kyoto	52
Kiyomizu-dera Jōju-in	清		水	寺	1-chome, Kiyomizu, Kyoto	15
Kōetsu-ji	光		悦	寺	Koetsu-cho, Takagamine, Kyoto	37
Kohō-an	孤		篷	庵	Daitoku-ji compound (see Daitoku-ji)	47
Kōmyō-in	光		明	院	Tofuku-ji compound (see Tōfuku-ji)	13
Konchi-in	金		地	院	Nanzen-ji compound (see Nanzen-ji)	21
Kongōrin-ji	金	剛	輪	寺	Matsuoji, Hatasho-cho, Shiga Pref.	84
Konpuku-ji	金		福	寺	Saikata-cho, Ichijoji, Kyoto	27
Koshō-ji (Formerly Shūrin-ji)	興聖寺(旧秀隣寺)				Kosho-ji, Iwase, Kuchiki-cho, Shiga Pref.	81
Kōtō-in	高		桐	院	Daitoku-ji compound (see Daitoku-ji)	50
Kōzan-ji	高		山	寺	Toganoö-cho, Umegahata, Kyoto	64
Kyoto Gosho	京	都	御	所	Gyoen, Kyoto	42
Kyū-Ninomaru, Nagoya-jō	名古屋城旧二の丸				Kyu-Ninomaru, Naka-ku, Nagoya	105
Manpuku-ji	萬		福	寺	Masuda-cho, Masuda City, Shimane Pref.	101
Manshu-in	曼		殊	院	Takenouchi-cho, Ichijoji, Kyoto	28
Matsuo Jinja	松	尾	神	社	Hamano-cho, Yokaichi City, Shiga Pref.	83
Mōtsu-ji	毛		越	寺	Hiraizumi-cho, Nishiiwai-gun, Iwate Pref.	109
Murin-an	無		隣	庵	Kusakawa-cho, Nanzen-ji, Kyoto	22
Nanzen-in	南		禅	院	Nanzen-ji compound (see Nanzen-ji)	20
Nanzen-ji	南		禅	寺	Fukuji-cho, Nanzen-ji, Kyoto	20
Ninna-ji	仁		和	寺	Ouchi-cho, Omuro, Kyoto	58
Ni-no-maru, Nijō-jō	二 条 城 二 の 丸				Horikawa Nijo, Kyoto	41
Nishi Hongan-ji	西	本	願	寺	Horikawa-Shichijo-agaru, Kyoto	38, 39
Nison-in	二		尊	院	Chojin-cho, Nison-in-mae, Saga, Kyoto	62

Garden					Address	Page
Ōbai-in	黄	梅		院	Daitoku-ji compound (*see* Daitoku-ji)	*51*
Okayama Kōraku-en	岡	山	後 楽	園	Furugyo-cho, Okayama	97
Ōmi Kohō-an	近 江	孤	篷	庵	Ueno, Asai-cho, Shiga Pref.	90
Omote Senke	表	千		家	Ogawa Teranouchi-agaru, Kyoto	44
Onjō-ji	園	城		寺	Onjoji-cho, Otsu City, Shiga Pref.	79
Ōsawa-no-Ike	大	沢 の		池	Osawa-cho, Saga, Kyoto	59
Raikyū-ji	頼	久		寺	Raikyuji-cho, Takahashi City, Okayama Pref.	98
Rakuraku-en	楽	々		園	Konki-machi, Hikone City, Shiga Pref.	87
Reiun-in	霊	雲		院	Myoshin-ji compound (*see* Daishin-in)	56
Renge-ji	蓮	華		寺	Hachiman-cho, Takano, Kyoto	35
Rikugi-en	六	義		園	Fujimae-cho, Bunkyo-ku, Tokyo	108
Rinkyū-ji	林	丘		寺	Karasuma-cho, Shugakuin, Kyoto	29
Ritsu-in	律			院	Hon-machi, Sakamoto, Otsu City, Shiga Pref.	*81*
Ritsurin Park	栗	林	公	園	Ritsurin-cho, Takamatsu City, Kagawa Pref.	96
Rokuō-in	鹿	王		院	Kitahori-cho, Saga, Kyoto	61
Ryōan-ji	龍	安		寺	Goryoshita-machi, Ryoanji, Kyoto	53
Ryōgen-in	龍	源		院	Daitoku-ji compound (*see* Daitoku-ji)	*51*
Ryōsoku-in	両	足		院	Yamatooji Shijo-sagaru, Kyoto	16
Ryōtan-ji	龍	潭		寺	Daido, Furusawa-cho, Hikone City, Shiga Pref.	*88, 89*
Saihō-ji (Moss Temple)	西	芳		寺	Jingadani-cho, Matsuo, Kyoto	*66, 67*
Saimyō-ji	西	明		寺	Ikedera, Kora-cho, Shiga Pref.	85
Sanbō-in	三	宝		院	Higashioji-cho, Daigo, Kyoto	73
Sangen-in	三	玄		院	Daitoku-ji compound (*see* Daitoku-ji)	*51*
Sanzen-in	三	千		院	Raigoin-cho, Ohara, Kyoto	*33*
Seigan-ji	青	岸		寺	Maibara, Maibara-cho, Shiga Pref.	89
Senshū-kaku, Tokushima-jō	徳 島 城	千 秋		閣	Tokushima Castle, Tokushima	94
Sentō Gosho	仙	洞	御	所	Gyoen, Kyoto	*43*
Shido-dera	志	度		寺	Shido-cho, Kagawa Pref.	95
Shinju-an	真	珠		庵	Daitoku-ji compound (*see* Daitoku-ji)	46
Shisen-dō	詩	仙		堂	Monguchi-cho, Ichijoji, Kyoto	26
Shōden-ji	正	伝		寺	Chinjuan-cho, Nishigamo, Kyoto	35
Shōju Raigō-ji	聖 衆	来	迎	寺	Hietsuji, Sakamoto-cho, Otsu City, Shiga Pref.	80
Shōren-in	青	蓮		院	Sanjobo-cho, Awataguchi, Kyoto	17
Shūgakuin Rikyū	修 学	院	離	宮	Karasuma-cho, Shugakuin, Kyoto	*30, 31*
Shūon-an	酬	恩		庵	Tanabe-cho, Kyoto Pref.	75
Taizō-in	退	蔵		院	Myoshin-ji compound (*see* Daishin-in)	55
Tenryū-ji	天	龍		寺	Susuki-no-baba-cho, Saga, Kyoto	60
Tōfuku-ji	東	福		寺	15-chome, Honmachi, Kyoto	*10, 11*
Tōji-in	等	持		院	Kita-machi, Tojiin, Kyoto	54